LATINO COMMUNITIES
EMERGING VOICES
POLITICAL, SOCIAL, CULTURAL, AND LEGAL ISSUES

Edited by

Antoinette Sedillo Lopez
University of New Mexico

A ROUTLEDGE SERIES

LATINO COMMUNITIES: EMERGING VOICES
POLITICAL, SOCIAL, CULTURAL, AND LEGAL ISSUES

ANTOINETTE SEDILLO LOPEZ, *General Editor*

LEAVING LATINOS OUT OF HISTORY
Teaching U.S. History in Texas

Julio Noboa

Routledge
New York & London

Published in 2006 by
Routledge
Taylor & Francis Group
270 Madison Avenue
New York, NY 10016

Published in Great Britain by
Routledge
Taylor & Francis Group
2 Park Square
Milton Park, Abingdon
Oxon OX14 4RN

Printed in the United States of America on acid-free paper
10 9 8 7 6 5 4 3 2 1

International Standard Book Number-10: 0-415-97586-7 (Hardcover)
International Standard Book Number-13: 978-0-415-97586-5 (Hardcover)
Library of Congress Card Number 2005019512

Library of Congress Cataloging-in-Publication Data

Noboa, Julio.
  Leaving Latinos out of history : teaching U.S. history in Texas / by Julio Noboa.
      p. cm. -- (Latino communities)
  Includes bibliographical references and index.
  ISBN 0-415-97586-7
    1. Hispanic Americans--Study and teaching--Texas. 2. Minorities--Study and teaching--Texas. 3. United States--History--Study and teaching--Texas. 4. Racism in textbooks--Texas. 5. Textbook bias--Texas. 6. Texas--Ethnic relations. 7. Texas--Race relations. I. Title. II. Series.

F395.S75N63 2005
976.4'00468--dc22   2005019512

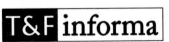

**Visit the Taylor & Francis Web site at
http://www.taylorandfrancis.com**

**and the Routledge Web site at
http://www.routledge-ny.com**

This book is dedicated
to my parents, Julio Noboa Gonzalez,
and Simonita Polanco Noboa,
who inculcated enduring values within me.

To my wife, Elsa Duarte-Noboa,
who inspired, challenged and
encouraged me from beginning to end.

To my three children,
Julio Alejandro, Sofia Rebecca, and Cassandra Lizette,
who taught me that parents are the first teachers.

And to the children and youth of Texas
who have yet to learn
the Latino legacy of our heritage.

Contents

Acknowledgments

This book was facilitated, guided and inspired by many teachers and mentors at every level of my formal and informal education. Several professors at the University of Texas at Austin both within and outside the Department of Curriculum and Instruction made invaluable contributions to the ultimate quality and significance of my investigation. Most of all, I am very grateful to the UTA faculty who served in my doctoral dissertation committee: José E. Limón, Maggie Rivas-Rodriquez, Mary Lee Webeck, and most particularly, Sherry L. Field who helped guide me through the final critical stages of this effort. Most especially, I am grateful to Mary S. Black, who provided wisdom and affirmation from the very beginning to my final completion.

Much encouragement, ideas and support were also my good fortune to receive from colleagues at the University of Northern Iowa, especially Christine Canning, with whom I had the opportunity to work closely for nearly a decade. Finally, several newer colleagues at the University of Texas at Brownsville helped with specific ideas and suggestions, including Renee Rubin, Manuel Medrano, and most specifically, Teresa Cadena, my editor, who assisted me at every level with the final development of this book.

My most heartfelt thanks to all of them, as well as to the willing participants in my investigations, the history teachers of Northside I.S.D., who generously opened up to me and freely expressed their minds on matters of profound importance to the education of coming generations.

Preface

Only after having lived in Texas for several years did I fully realize how much there is to know about this huge and heterogeneous state. As a Puerto Rican, living and working in Chicago, Illinois for most of my life, I had many preconceived notions about this southwestern state and its people. Yet during two decades, though a few of the stereotypes I had about Texas were reinforced, most were completely shattered. Among my many surprising discoveries was just how deeply the Mexican ethos was engrained in the most profound roots of Texan culture.

To begin with, there is an entire ranching lifestyle that practically defines what is Texan. It is the lifestyle in which the indefatigable image of the Great American Cowboy of silver screen and folk legend was forged and fostered. Yet, most Americans don't even know that it is a way of life inherited from the centuries-old ranching culture of *vaqueros, charros,* and *rancheros* of Northern Mexico, especially in the province of *Tejas.*

It took me several years to fully understand that the Mexicans I saw with cowboy hats who called themselves *Tejano,* were not simply a Latino imitation of the American cowboy, they were in fact the cowboys being imitated. Even more significantly, in all my years of formal schooling I had never learned about this vaquero-cowboy connection; I discovered this from my own personal reading and observation.

Yet this Mexican element was not only the foundation for that defining cowboy culture of Texas; it was a quality reflected in the Spanish names of cities, towns and counties, as well as in the flavor of the state's characteristic cuisine, music, and dance. All these features bespeak of the traditions established long ago by the earliest Mexican pioneers and settlers. Still today, many of these traditions are not only perpetuated by their Mexican American descendents, but also by the millions of immigrants from other states, regions, and nations who have made Texas their home.

Looking beyond the traditional historical past at contemporary times, I discovered that it has been in Texas that Mexican Americans have established national organizations, generated movements, and developed leaders who have gained them a measure of political power unmatched in any other state of the union. The Latino presence may be just as old in California and New Mexico, it may be just as profound in Florida and New York, but it can be argued that it is in Texas where Latinos, particularly Mexican Americans, have the strongest and longest convergence of history, culture, and political power.

Considering this historically entrenched Latino presence in Texas, one would expect therefore, that when millions of Texas public school children and youth learn about the history of their state and nation, Latino related names, events, movements, and perspectives would be part of the narrative. Unfortunately this is not the case. In fact, Latinos are usually absent, marginalized or stereotyped in the telling of the story of Texas and of our nation.

The 2000 Census only confirmed what many scholars, educators, and policy makers had already recognized: Latinos have become the largest minority group in our nation, and long before that, in Texas. Yet, when Americans visit the video store, the cineplex, a bookstore, or when they turn on the television, they could easily get the impression that Latinos are a tiny minority with an insignificant presence.

For decades, reputable and credible scholars have documented that Latinos are blatantly underrepresented in the most pervasive and powerful mass media of America. Among the many implications of this exclusion is the general public's ignorance about Latinos and about who they really are in their wide diversity of national origins, racial mixtures and cultural identities.

This ignorance creates, almost by default, a tremendous burden of responsibility for our system of public education to provide what the mass media does not: namely accurate, objective and relevant information about America's largest ethnic group, raising the inevitable question: *To what extent do our public schools fulfill the general public's need for more relevant and accurate information about Latinos?*

Given its particular heritage, Texas provided an ideal location for a case study in which to conduct an investigation on how that quintessential narrative about our common heritage, namely United States history, is taught to millions of children and youth. One of the earliest key discoveries I made was that, given the size of its market and the intensity of its partisan advocates, Texas exerts an extraordinary national influence on textbook selection, curriculum standards, and standardized testing.

Thus, the major purpose of this multifaceted investigation was to discover the extent to which Latinos are represented in our national historical narrative as presented in Texas public schools, and to ascertain the relative quantity and quality of that representation.

In order to gain a comprehensive portrait of Latino representation in the teaching of U.S. history in Texas, I explored four key distinct areas: The Texas Essential Knowledge and Skills (TEKS), textbooks, teaching, and testimony.

The TEKS curriculum standards establish a foundation for curriculum content, classroom instruction, high-stakes testing, teacher training, and textbook adoption. I conducted a content analysis of the TEKS as well as of five textbooks officially adopted by the State Board of Education that fulfill all the TEKS standards. Three of these textbooks had already been officially adopted by the state and used for a decade; the other two textbooks were adopted for use for the decade to come.

Additionally, I identified through a series of interviews and a focus group, the specific topics teachers chose to cover when teaching U.S. history at both the middle and high school levels, as well as the reasons why the teachers made these content choices. Finally, I accessed the public record to examine the issues, concerns, suggestions, and corrections expressed by groups and individuals regarding the representation of Latinos in U.S. history textbooks during the 2002 public hearings in Austin, Texas.

The methods and data generated from each of these four inter-related areas of study will be presented in separate chapters. The final chapter will discuss the implications of these findings as interpreted in the context of theoretical perspectives and related research.

The ultimate results of this multifaceted investigation may not be surprising to those who are well aware of Latino underrepresentation, from television to textbooks. However, these findings do provide cogent and compelling documentation as well as incontrovertible evidence of a serious gap in the history curriculum of Texas and very likely, of most other states in our nation.

It is a public education problem that can only be resolved by the deliberate will of dedicated educators at every level of public schooling. I hope this book will help inspire them to make an intentional effort to present a full and accurate account of our nation's historical narrative without leaving Latinos out.

Introduction

The Teaching of History

An interesting yet divisive debate has long existed in our country about how history is taught in our public schools. Part of this interest is based on the indisputable importance attached to learning history in every society, especially in modern, complex, industrial societies, where a shared sense of history is considered essential for social cohesion (Levine, 1996; Loewen, 1995; Nash, Crabtree, & Dunn, 1997; Schlesinger, 1991).

The well-founded and documented fact that the upcoming generations of students are not gaining an adequate level of knowledge and understanding of our nation's history augments this concern. Since the 1983 National Commission on Excellence report, *A Nation at Risk,* several books and research reports have decried this problem. Among them, E.D. Hirsch's best selling book, *Cultural Literacy,* claimed that students were not obtaining the common store of knowledge that makes communication and social cohesion possible (Hirsch, 1987).

The First National Assessment of History and Literature issued a report in 1983, *What Do Our 17-Year-Olds Know?,* which revealed the results of an assessment test given to 8,000 students nationwide. The average score on the test which covered the basic facts of American history was only 55% correct answers. Then in 1990, the National Assessment of Educational Progress (NAEP), the "Nation's Report Card," published the results of their first comprehensive test on American history given to 16,000 students. Among their findings: only 5% of high school seniors taking the test could interpret more challenging historical ideas and information (Nash, et al., 1997, p. 109–10).

The *NAEP 1994 U.S. History Report Card* was of a study of students' achievement levels in U.S. history in grades 4, 8, and 12. This National Assessment of Educational Progress reported that only 17% of fourth graders, 14% of eighth graders and 11% of twelfth graders reached the *Proficient* achievement level. Although at grades 4 and 8, over 60% of students reached the *Basic* achievement level, fewer than half of grade 12 students had demonstrated this ability (Beatty, et al., 1996, p. xi).

The more recent Nation's Report Card, *US History 2001,* showed more fourth and eighth grade students reaching *Proficient* levels in 2001 than in 1994; however, the performance of twelfth graders remained stable. As in 1994, only 11% of high school seniors performed at or above the *Proficient* level, whereas 18% of the fourth-graders, and 17% of eighth graders achieved that level. Despite increases at two grade levels, even among those who had the highest scores, students who achieved *Proficient* levels still represent less than one-fifth of the test-takers (Lapp, Grigg, & Tay-Lim, 2002).

TEXTBOOKS, DIVERSITY AND THE CULTURE WARS

In addition to the above concerns, the importance of teaching history has intensified over the last few decades because educators, scholars and leaders have focused on issues of diversity and especially on the exclusion of minorities and women from our nation's historical narrative. An entire multicultural education movement has developed and grown, generating a powerful political and intellectual reaction from conservatives. Multicultural education has become a controversial topic of often-acrimonious public debate affecting all levels of education (Banks, 1997; D'Souza, 1991; Levine, 1996; Nieto, 1992; Schlesinger, 1991).

Energizing this debate on cultural diversity in the classroom is the relative absence or underrepresentation of minorities, and particularly Latinos in social studies textbooks. Since 1949, when the American Council on Education (ACE) conducted the first major study of over 300 textbooks, and into the mid 1990s, many studies have documented and confirmed that women and minorities have been relatively excluded or marginalized in social studies textbooks (Committee on the Study of Teaching Materials in Intergroup Relations, 1949; Garcia, 1993).

The thorny issue of how minorities and women are represented in the curriculum has become one of the most intense debates in our nation, often fueled by politics and ideology. This is especially controversial for history textbooks (Garcia, 1993; Lerner, Nagai, & Rothman, 1995; Loewen, 1995; Nash & Dunn, 1995; Schlesinger, 1991).

Four decades after the ACE study scholars noted discernible increases in the quantity and diversity of minority representation. However, there had not been a dramatic improvement in the quality of that treatment in terms of depth and objectivity (Garcia & Goebel, 1985; Garcia, 1993).

Aside from the specific textbook treatments of Latinos and other minorities, there has long been a keen and controversial interest in the content and quality of textbooks per se (Apple & Christian-Smith, 1991; Sleeter & Grant, 1991). Although the actual role that textbooks play in the classroom has also been of some attention and dispute, most educational researchers and historians agree that textbooks establish a foundation for what is considered valuable, relevant, useful, or even official knowledge (Apple & Christian-Smith, 1991; Rigberg, 1991). For decades our nation and others the world over have recognized the centrality of textbooks in the entire process and politics of public schooling.

Nowhere in the curriculum is the influence of divergent and often antagonistic views more evident than in the social studies, and particularly in history. It is in the telling of history that a people or nation synthesize the values, aspirations, struggles and experiences which are worthy of memory and recognition. It is perhaps, the most complete and comprehensive piece of cultural legacy that one generation attempts to leave for the next.

Although originating within education and academia, the heated political debates over such approaches as bilingual education, multiculturalism, and Afrocentrism reveal just how easily these issues spill over into the public domain, often without the benefit of reasoned analyses. And so it is with textbooks.

Well-funded and organized fundamentalist Christian groups, such as Mel and Norma Gabler's Educational Research Analysts, the National Association of Christian Educators, and Citizens for Excellence in Education have for decades wielded influence at every key level of textbook adoption in Texas and other major states. Textbook publishers must negotiate with conservatives today, as they had to in the 1970s with more liberal-progressive groups. Among those focusing on textbook issues at that time was the Council for Interracial Books for Children (CIBC) that alerted parents and educators about the negative treatment of minorities in textbooks (Garcia, 1993).

As part of the larger "Culture Wars" about values, diversity, and "political correctness," the issue of including women and racial/ethnic minorities in history curricula and textbooks has also generated much journalistic commentary and spilled over into the arena of public opinion (Gonzales & Rodriguez, 1998; Stille, 1998; Wilentz, 1997).

More significantly, a body of scholarly research has also been produced, much of it qualitative, but with considerable quantitative data, that focuses primarily on the representation of women and African Americans in history textbooks (Garcia, 1993). Not as frequently or as thoroughly investigated, however, is how Latinos, Asians, Native Americans, and even some White ethnics are portrayed and presented in textbooks read by millions of students (Garcia, 1980, 1993).

Nevertheless, the textbook treatment of Latinos in particular has been more thoroughly researched over the last two decades, especially in the area of social studies and U.S. history (Garcia, 1980; Salvucci, 1991; Sleeter & Grant, 1991). Researchers have found that in some texts, African Americans and American Indians received more attention than did Hispanics and Asian Americans (Glazar & Ueda, 1983). Hispanics in particular, and the pivotal events which mark their history in the United States, have been omitted, misrepresented, and stereotyped in textbooks published even during the decades (1970s—1990s) in which their national presence was being more widely recognized (Arries, 1994; Cook, 1985; de Varona, 1989; Garcia, 1980; Sleeter & Grant, 1991).

In a more recent study, Cruz (2002) analyzed the content of history textbooks at the fifth grade level as well as at the eighth and eleventh grade levels when U.S. history is taught. Cruz noted and compared the representation of both Latino and Latin Americans among these, the "most popular and state-adopted" textbooks used in Florida, another state with a large and influential Hispanic population, and found that:

> Despite recent efforts, initiatives, and legislation mandating multicultural and global perspectives in education . . . The findings of this study overwhelmingly conclude that Latinos and Latin Americans are frequently omitted form the story of the United States and are often depicted in pejorative and stereotypical ways (Cruz, 2002, p. 336).

The need to provide history students with reliable information about Hispanics is underscored by the phenomenal growth of this population, especially in the last decade. The 2000 Census confirmed that the 35.3 million Hispanics in the U.S. constitute over 12.5% of the general population. This surpasses, for the first time in history, the number of African Americans in our nation and represents for Latinos an increase of nearly 60% from the 1990 census (Zabarenko, 2001). Among the significant changes noted by demographers is that Latino populations are no longer limited to the larger states such as Texas, California, and New York, but are now showing unprecedented growth in cities and small towns of Midwestern and Southern states such as Iowa and Georgia (Christian Science Monitor, 2001).

Finally it is important to consider that, along with other states with significant minority populations like California and Florida, Texas is one of the largest and most influential markets for textbook adoption in the nation (Apple & Christian-Smith, 1991; Salvucci, 1991; Sewall, 1998).

TEKS: CURRICULUM STANDARDS FOR SOCIAL STUDIES

These demographic realities have long been predicted and even anticipated by some policy makers and textbook publishers. However, the extent to which this "Browning of America" has influenced the development of curriculum standards for the social studies varies from state to state.

Over the last fifteen years, since about the mid-1980s, many states have joined the effort to establish standards in the social studies. Among them are larger states with significant Latino populations including New York, California, Illinois and Texas. The impetus for establishing educational standards was generated in 1990 with the adoption of National Education Goals by President George Bush and the National Governors' Association. President Bill Clinton signed these goals into law in March 1994 in the Goals 2000, Educate America Act (Nash & Crabtree, 1996). The very concept of establishing standards found broad support among the American people, as well as elected officials from both political parties at every level.

In Texas, the standards movement took several forms, most notably the development of a new curriculum, the *Texas Essential Knowledge and Skills* or TEKS, which represented the first curriculum revision by the Texas Education Agency (TEA) in over ten years.

For every TEKS content area, a diverse team of teachers, parents, college faculty, curriculum specialists and business people were selected to produce the written standards. The social studies writing team consisted of thirty-five members with twenty-one Euroamericans, nine Hispanics, four African Americans and one American Indian. Seventeen of them were teachers while the rest included six social studies coordinators, five instructional administrators, four university academics, two parents and one business person (TEA, 1997b).

Notwithstanding extensive citizen involvement, or perhaps as a direct result of it, there was very intense controversy surrounding the establishment of TEKS, especially in the areas of social studies, notably history. Dividing the State Board of Education along traditional conservative vs. liberal perspectives, the TEKS controversy caused several delays and rewrites in social studies, and other subject areas. State board of education members Joseph Bernal and Robert Offutt, for example, openly expressed opposing viewpoints on the TEKS and their process of adoption (Bernal, 1997; Offutt, 1997).

Even a national figure, Diane Ravitch, former Assistant U.S. Secretary of Education and veteran of the culture wars, got involved. She visited with TEA staff members and made proposed improvements to the TEKS curriculum. She also remarked on how the rewrite in the TEKS could affect the selection of curriculum and textbooks across the nation considering that other states look to Texas as an example. "That gives Texas more importance than any other state in the country" (quoted in Ramos, 1997a).

After much discussion and debate, due in large measure to the fundamental importance accorded to TEKS for teaching, testing, textbook selection and teacher training, it was officially approved on July 11, 1997. Today, educational policy and practice in Texas is guided by the curricular standards established in TEKS, designed to "serve as a basis for instructional materials, state assessments, and educator preparation and development" (TEA, 1996, p. i).

Less than a year passed before the Thomas B. Fordham Foundation, a Washington D.C. think tank, in 1998 ranked Texas' history and geography curriculum among the best in the nation. Texas, along with Colorado and Indiana received an "A" grade in Geography standards and a "B" grade in History standards, as did California and Massachusetts. Virginia received the only "A" grade in history, but obtained only a "D" in geography. Texas was the only state to receive an A and B grade in both social studies areas. "Texas was held up as the example," declared Matt Mauer, spokesman for the Fordham Foundation (Hoholik, 1998).

Thus, it seems that in the arena of social studies standards, Texas has obtained national recognition for the clarity, content, and comprehensiveness of its TEKS. However, the extent to which this reputation is warranted in relation to TEKS' treatment of Latinos and other minorities is still an open question.

THE TEACHER AS GATEKEEPER

Despite the obvious influence of established state curriculum standards, and the impact this has on textbook selection, it is at the classroom level that students actually engage with the curriculum. That applied curriculum, and the particular content and approaches used to deliver it, is invariably determined by the individual classroom history teacher.

Several studies have documented the important role history teachers play in selecting content, using instructional methods, and utilizing educational materials including textbooks, maps, and audiovisuals. These and other investigations have also identified some of the factors which influence history teachers' curricular and instructional decisions, including structural conditions in the school, community and student characteristics, as well as their own beliefs, values, social class, knowledge, and training.

For example, in terms of content choice, a 1989–90 survey conducted by the National Center for History in the Schools at UCLA, found that high school U.S. history teachers spend more classroom time teaching about the twentieth century than the earlier history of the nation. Also, while few were frequent users of such materials as bibliographies, documents, or literature of the period, the main teaching tool for most of the 481 participating teachers was the survey textbook (Thomas, 1992). Since the history teacher is a pivotal decision-maker in what is ultimately taught and how, a full comprehension of how U.S. history is taught must also include a better understanding of the teachers' role as curricular content gatekeeper.

FUNDAMENTAL RESEARCH QUESTIONS

Considering the multiple factors involved in the teaching of U.S. History in Texas, as discussed above, I decided that a mixed methods approach would be most appropriate. As a result, several interrelated research questions, each pertinent to its specific component study of the investigation, direct this investigation. Despite its multifaceted approach, this effort and its objectives are guided by one single fundamental question: *What is the relative quantity and quality of Latino inclusion and representation in the teaching of U.S. history in the public schools of Texas?*

Although this question cannot be fully and definitively answered by this exploratory investigation, it does serve to generate a corpus of useful data and some analyses that contribute towards formulating a more complete and accurate response to this vital question.

Additionally, five other interrelated questions more specific to the component studies of this multi-faceted inquiry will be considered:

1. Whereas Texas has obtained national recognition for the clarity, content, and comprehensiveness of its TEKS, to what extent do these standards reflect a complete, inclusive and comprehensive view of our nation's multicultural history, and of the Latino presence within it?

2. Given the influence of Texas on the standards and selection of textbooks in the national market, to what extent are Latinos represented in the U.S. history textbooks adopted in that very state wherein they have had the most intense cultural history and significant influence?

3. Whereas it is the U.S. history teacher who ultimately decides what content is covered in the classroom, what are the factors that influence these content choices?

4. Given that U.S. history teachers content choices are influenced by several factors, which of these interact to help or hinder the inclusion of Latinos in the classroom curriculum?

5. Given that U.S. history textbook selection is a very politicized and ideological process involving a multitude of issues, what kinds of issues directly related to Latino representation were expressed in the discourse and testimony of the public hearings?

PURPOSES

The ultimate purpose of this investigation was to identify, explore and gain an understanding of those factors that affect the extent to which Latinos are integrated into the historical narrative of the classroom. Qualitative methods were applied by way of personal interviews and a focus group with U.S. history teachers. The textbook adoption process was explored through the analysis of public testimony and participant observation. Other studies consisted of detailed content analyses of textbooks and curriculum standards as well as course content surveys related to the teaching of U.S. history.

Relevant findings from four component studies were combined to provide a more holistic documentation on the representation of Latinos in the teaching of U.S. history in Texas. The areas investigated included:

a) the Texas Essential Knowledge and Skills curriculum standards (TEKS);
b) current and recently adopted textbooks;
c) the perspectives and practices of teachers; and
d) the textbook adoption process and related testimony.

These various studies were integrated into the overall design of the larger investigation and into the analysis of its data. Though each study had a purpose specific to its particular focus, each contributed towards constructing a general mosaic of interrelated parts which taken together advance the ultimate objective of the larger investigation.

For example, the major purpose of the study on the Texas Essential Knowledge and Skills (TEKS) was to determine the quantity and quality of Latino presence in these curriculum standards and to compare and contrast that to how African Americans and American Indians are represented (Noboa, 2000c). Given the demographic, political, historical and cultural realities of Texas, it was useful to determine the extent to which ethnoracial minorities and especially Latinos, are mentioned and/or represented in the content of U.S. history curriculum standards of the TEKS. It was also significant because the TEKS are used as a basis for selecting textbooks, designing standardized tests, training teachers, and instructing students (TEA, 1996, p. i).

The purpose of the textbook study was to determine how and to what extent Latinos in general as well as the three largest Hispanic groups—Mexican-Americans, Puerto Ricans, and Cuban-Americans—are represented in the most widely used U.S. history textbooks in the state of Texas. While seeking to quantify the amount of Latino representation in these texts, this research also investigated the qualitative extent to which that representation is accurate, objective and complete (Noboa, 2000b).

The research on the U.S. history textbook adoption process in Texas during 2002 was designed to document the critiques regarding Latino representation in U.S. history textbooks from the oral and written testimony. It also included a comparison and contrast of Latino representation in two recently adopted textbooks. Most importantly, it provided another opportunity to become intimately engaged as a participant observer in the most recent adoption process for social studies (Noboa, 2003a).

Given its strategic history, accessibility, cultural heritage, as well as predominant Hispanic presence, I decided that San Antonio, the Alamo City, would be an ideal location to conduct my case study of history teachers. The purpose of the personal interviews with U.S. history teachers was to examine their beliefs and perceptions regarding the content of their courses. Also examined were some of the factors that impact this content and how these relate to teachers' content choices. Special attention was focused as well on the extent to which, and the context in which, participants mention the inclusion of women, minorities, and especially Latinos in the classroom curriculum (Noboa, 2000a).

A second component of the study on teaching involved a focus group of history teachers, generating further exploration of the factors that influence content choices made by U.S. history teachers. This helped me gain a better understanding of those influences that determine the extent to which ethnic and racial minorities, especially Latinos, are integrated into the classroom's historical narrative (Noboa, 2003b).

The ultimate objective of this multifaceted approach was for these four studies to work together in concert in an attempt to provide a more holistic view of how U.S. history is taught in Texas and to help reveal some of the patterns of representation or exclusion specifically related to Latinos and to other racial/ethnic minorities in the state's curriculum for U.S. history.

METHODS

As stated above, this mixed methods investigation consisted of several, mostly qualitative approaches, namely personal interviews, focus groups, and participant observation. Content analyses were also used for textbooks, testimony, curriculum standards and course content checklists.

Personal interviews were conducted with twelve US history teachers, mostly in their classrooms at the end of the school day. The participants were selected because they were articulate, outstanding teachers who had a variety of backgrounds and experience. Participants included both men and women representing the three major ethnoracial groups in the city: Anglo, Latino and African American. They included both middle and high school teachers as well as teachers with decades of experience, and others with only a few years. The interviews were audiotaped and their responses were analyzed.

The focus group consisted of four male US history teachers, representing all three ethnoracial groups who had a wide variety of teaching experiences, but also quite articulate and opinionated. This focus group session was audiotaped and later transcribed for analysis.

Participants of both the personal interviews and the focus groups completed a course content checklist indicating the frequency with which they covered certain individuals, groups, concepts, or events in class. These checklists were analyzed to reveal, more specifically, which of the topics were the most and least covered.

The participant observation approach was used during the Texas textbook adoption process of 2002, when I obtained information and guidelines and actually participated in the public hearings, providing testimony before the Texas Board of Education. I also observed the process from that perspective, taking the opportunity to meet, converse with and establish rapport with other individuals and organizations providing testimony that day. Becoming an actor within the process permitted this researcher to better understand not only the public testimony process itself, but also the concerns, perceptions and motivations of other participants, especially the Latinos who participated or were present.

The content analyses for both the eighth grade and high school level courses were conducted on several key documents related to the teaching of U.S. history in Texas. First among them, the Texas Essential Knowledge and

Skills (TEKS) curriculum guidelines were analyzed for the relative presence of Latinos, African Americans and American Indians, specifically among the groups and individuals actually mentioned by name.

The contents of U.S. history textbooks were analyzed for the quantity and the quality of Latino representation. Three major textbooks recently used in the last decade were thoroughly analyzed in terms of the number of pages as well as the accuracy and objectivity of the Latino-related content. Two other textbooks up for adoption in 2003 were also analyzed for quantity and quality, but in more general terms, using a contrast-comparison approach.

Finally, to identify the kinds of issues being raised by groups and individuals, content analysis was used to review the testimony regarding Latino representation provided during the 2002 textbook adoption process.

Much of the validity of this particular mixed method investigation will emerge from the data itself. Greater validity is demonstrated from having consistent or comparable ideas, concerns, issues, and perspectives emerge from various sources such as interviews, focus groups, and public testimonies. The extent to which the findings from the content analyses of textbooks and TEKS, for example, reflect or support the findings derived through different methods, can be one clear indication of this investigation's validity.

MY INITIAL ASSUMPTIONS

Based on personal experience as well as formal interviews and informal conversations about schooling with Latinos from many occupations and professions, I had formed several assumptions. The first was that Latinos would likely be underrepresented in the curriculum. I also assumed that racial and ethnic minorities in general would not be fairly represented in social studies teaching, although it was also expected that of all the groups, African Americans would be the most or the best represented in textbooks, curriculum guidelines, and other curriculum materials. Other assumptions concerned the role of teachers as gatekeepers of classroom knowledge and specifically that many would express having some conflict with adopted textbooks or with established curricula, standards, or high-stakes testing.

These initial assumptions were tested through the variety of research approaches employed. All of them were confirmed by the data gathered from this investigation, yet as will be discussed later, the research also generated a wealth of data that provides insight and understanding far beyond the scope of my initial assumptions.

SIGNIFICANCE OF THE INVESTIGATION

Several key demographic and educational realities lend significance to this investigation, the phenomenal growth and the wide distribution of Latinos throughout the nation as documented by the 2000 Census being a primary factor. As Latinos are no longer limited to certain regions of the nation nor are they concentrated only in the large cities, other Americans will increasingly be attending school with Latinos or working in some professional or occupational capacity with Latinos as supervisors, colleagues or clients.

Latinos, and especially the largest Latino national origin group, Mexican Americans, have had a long history of residence, cultural influence and political activity in this nation. However, the general American public is often unaware or very misinformed about Latinos. Although not as blatantly as in past decades, there still persist numerous negative and demeaning stereotypes of Latinos mostly perpetrated by print and electronic media. While these portrayals have been challenged in recent years, the most powerful media continues to significantly exclude Latinos, and underrepresent their presence and influence in our nation's society, history and culture.

The combination of these two realities—the fact that Latinos are now the largest minority group in the nation and that they are systematically underrepresented in the media—places an enormous responsibility on the educational system. Aside from the many challenges already burdening public education, especially in the area of Latino education (high drop out rates, poor achievement, low test scores, etc.), there is also the unanticipated challenge of potentially being the most reliable source on Latinos for the general American public. Since the film industry, television, newspapers, magazines and, until quite recently, book publishers have all done a dismal job of educating the American public about Latinos, it unfortunately falls to an already overburdened public school system to somehow fill this information gap.

Discovering the extent to which our educational system is doing so is the driving force energizing this effort. For this reason, this investigation focuses on U.S. history, the master narrative for our nation's social studies, and how it is taught in a state that has one of the most historical and significant Latino presences. It also examines how history teachers in a city such as San Antonio, with a long history of Latino political organization and cultural development, include Latino topics in the classroom.

Going beyond mere anecdotal information, this investigation documents the representation of Latinos in the teaching of U.S. history in a state and city where their presence and influence is already well recognized and undeniable. One implication is clear: If Latinos are underrepresented in the history curriculum of a state and city wherein they have arguably the greatest concentration of presence and power, what can be expected of other states or regions of our nation?

Given that Texas is now serving as a model for curriculum standards, especially in the area of social studies, and that it is also the model for the use of high stakes, standardized tests as the ultimate assessment tool for evaluating students, teachers, schools and even districts, it is imperative to document what effect these curriculum standards and testing have on the curriculum in general, and especially on the coverage of Latinos and minorities.

Texas is also a very important and influential state for the adoption of textbooks used throughout the nation, and the determination of their final printed content. Thus it is useful to document as well how Latinos are represented in the textbooks adopted in this state.

Finally, the significance of this study also draws from the decades-long "Culture Wars" (Nash, Crabtree & Dunn, 1997; Levine, 1996), most specifically, the struggle of women and minorities to be duly recognized in the historical and cultural narratives being expounded to millions of public school students throughout the nation. The debate over multiculturalism at every level of schooling has generated many alarmist books and acrimonious conflicts. Yet it has also stimulated maturity, growth and sound research among advocates and practitioners of multicultural education.

It is my hope that this investigation will provide useful data for those who seek to understand the attitudes, policies, and practices that hinder or help educators provide an accurate and objective representation of Latinos and other racial and ethnic minorities in the teaching of our nation's history.

MYSELF AS RESEARCHER

Born in New York City of immigrant Puerto Rican parents, I was raised in thoroughly bilingual and bicultural environments at home, in school and in my surrounding community. Moving to Chicago at a very young age, and attending that city's public schools from kindergarten through high school, also gave me opportunities to learn and develop my ideas and worldview in a multicultural, multi-racial, and multi-ethnic context.

That experience in diversity, especially in my schooling and in my various employment experiences, stimulated my interest in issues of cultural diversity and eventually led to my decision to major in anthropology at the University of Illinois in Chicago where I obtained a BA degree in that discipline. Later, I attended Northwestern University in Evanston, Illinois, where I completed graduate coursework in both anthropology and education, obtaining a Masters of Arts in Education.

As my formal education advanced, my employment opportunities were naturally enhanced, and I worked in the areas of educational advocacy, social service management, and educational administration, both in government agencies and in non-profit community based organizations. Most of these experiences offered, to a greater or lesser extent, opportunities to conduct investigations, in collaboration with my colleagues, regarding the issues, conditions, problems and resources that existed in predominantly Latino schools and communities of Chicago.

After moving to San Antonio, Texas in the mid 1980s, I worked in drug prevention education at the elementary school level. In this capacity, mostly based on research of available resources and community characteristics, I designed and implemented a curriculum tailored for Mexican American students at a low-income inner-city public school. Later, working for another organization, Communities-in-Schools, I conducted a review of the literature on dropout prevention and managed a program at the middle and high school levels.

My most extensive experience with educational research was at the Tomás Rivera Center (TRC), integrated at that time within Trinity University. Serving as research writer, and later as research editor, I worked closely with scholars, predominantly in the area of educational policy as it affects the Latino communities at the local, state and national levels. In consultation with demographers, sociologists, and educational policy experts, I helped edit and sometimes write reports, policy papers, and legislative briefs.

At the TRC, I also had the opportunity of conducting research on the status of immigrant students in Texas and wrote a report published by the Center, *They come to learn: Hispanic immigrant students in Texas* (Noboa-Polanco, 1991). That same year I also collaborated with a history professor at Trinity University, Linda Salvucci, in the analysis and critique of adopted textbook representations of Mexico, Mexicans, and Mexican Americans. Each of us wrote a paper and provided testimony regarding our findings to the Texas State Board of Education (Salvucci, 1991; Noboa, 1991a).

Having experienced the adoption process and observed it closely as a participant allowed me to gather data and gain insights on how the process works and the extent to which political and religious ideology play significant roles within it. This enabled me to write a paper on this topic, *The Textbook adoption process in Texas: Social studies and cultural diversity*, and present it at the Southwestern Social Science Association conference that year (Noboa, 1991b).

The following year was a pivotal one for the adoption of textbooks in Texas, especially in the subject areas of English and Social Studies. Drawing from my experience with the public testimony process, I collaborated with a group of predominantly Latino scholars, historians, and educators, as well as college and eighth grade students. Under the name of MASA, the *Multicultural Alliance of San Antonio,* we reviewed and provided public testimony on several English and history textbooks in the context of their coverage of women and minorities, but especially of Latino groups, individuals and historical events (Texas Education Agency, 1992). Based on these experiences, and using some of the data generated from the efforts of MASA, I gathered enough information from a variety of sources to write a paper and present it at the 1993 conference of the Society for Applied Anthropology on how textbooks portrayed women, minorities and Latinos (Noboa, 1993).

The next year, I began working with the University of Northern Iowa as an instructor and clinical supervisor. Being in this capacity for over nine years, allowed me ample opportunities to conduct classroom observations and provide cross-cultural teacher training. My colleague, Christine Canning, and I often reflected on the challenges of preparing Anglo student teachers from Iowa to instruct effectively in classrooms with predominantly Latino and other racially, ethnically and socially diverse students. From these reflections and from qualitative data we collected, we wrote and presented two papers on relevant themes and presented them at teacher education conferences (Canning & Noboa, 1997; Canning, Noboa & Salazar-Guenther, 2002).

During the last few years, while working on my doctoral studies, I have also had opportunities to conduct a variety of investigations, most notably a study on the curriculum and school climate at Lanier High School during World War II. Located in the traditional Mexican American barrio of San Antonio's west side, Lanier High School served as a fruitful site for research. Combining district archival records, yearbooks, newspapers, and interviews with former students, I was able to create a historic and contextualized portrait of Lanier. Originally presented at a conference on Latinos in World War II, this paper was revised and expanded and has now been published as a chapter in the book, *Mexican Americans and World War II,* edited by Maggie Rivas-Rodriquez (Noboa, 2005).

Among other relevant topics I have investigated are Afrocentrism in U.S. schools, the debate over multiculturalism, and the effects of an Anglocentric curriculum on Latino students. My most recent and intense research activity, which will be more fully described in the subsequent chapters, is represented by the several component studies mentioned above that comprise this book.

Chapter One
The Research on Latinos and Minorities in the Curriculum

Several bodies of research, notably some on curriculum standards and the Texas Essential Knowledge and Skills discussed in the Introduction, have relevance to this investigation. Three bodies of literature most directly pertinent to this investigation will be reviewed in this chapter: 1) the textbook treatment of Latinos, racial and ethnic minorities, and women, 2) the role of classroom teachers and factors influencing their content choices, and 3) the rationales and approaches for multicultural education.

Also included is a brief overview of findings from two previous studies I conducted on relevant topics, concluding with a discussion of how both investigations established a foundation for this current effort.

LATINOS, MINORITIES AND WOMEN IN HISTORY TEXTBOOKS

The entire issue of racial and ethnic as well as gender representation in textbooks came to a political climax during the intense national debate surrounding the *National History Standards* first published in 1994. Gary B. Nash, Professor of History at UCLA, led the effort to develop a set of standards for both American and world history in response to gubernatorial, presidential and congressional mandates. However, upon their release, the standards were vigorously condemned as unAmerican, politically correct, and extremely revisionist by conservative critics led by Lynne Cheney and Rush Limbaugh (Nash & Dunn, 1995).

In their attempt to make credible some of the lies and misinformation being disseminated about the writers, content, and intent of these standards, conservative critics focused almost exclusively on the "examples of student achievement." In so doing, these critics counted names mentioned in the suggested and optional activities and incorrectly treated these examples as if they were part of a textbook. Based on these tallies, the critics then railed against the "excessive" inclusion of minorities and women at the expense of White males, despite the fact that most of the names mentioned in these examples were indeed White males. This national controversy and others regarding curriculum and textbooks in states such as New York, California and Texas illustrate the highly charged atmosphere that is always generated by a discussion of what should be taught in history classes.

Nevertheless, the foundations of this debate are rooted in a justifiable response to the negative and inaccurate way women and minorities have been depicted for decades in textbooks, especially before the 1960s. Jesus Garcia (1993) provides a brief historical overview of the prevailing policies and practices regarding textbook content beginning in the nineteenth century.

Back then, textbooks were written at a time, as William Reese put it, when "public schools taught children and then adolescents that America was Christian, republican, and the greatest nation on earth" (quoted in Garcia, 1993, p. 1). Writing in this context, textbook authors created an ideal fantasy world of heroes and villains where, according to Ruth Elson, "Individuals are to be understood in terms of easily discernible, inherent characteristics of their race and nationality as much as in terms of their individual character" (Ibid).

Schoolbook *Negroes* were depicted as foolish, childlike, and requiring supervision and providing assistance to Whites from their menial positions. American Indians were more often described as cruel, vengeful and barbarous than alert or brave. Latin Americans had all the bad qualities of the Spaniards, but none of their virtues such as courage, firmness or patience. Clear distinctions were also drawn between Northern and Western Europeans versus those from the East and South, with the best or most virtuous being those that most closely resemble the Anglo-American racial and cultural prototype (Garcia, 1993).

Little interest was demonstrated by researchers in the representation of minorities in textbooks during the first half of the twentieth century until 1949 when the American Council on Education sponsored the first major review published in this century (Committee on the Study of Teaching Materials in Intergroup Relations, 1949). The Committee examined over 300 textbooks used nationwide at all levels during the 1940s to determine their treatment of the topic of "intergroup relations."

Michael Kane (1970) reports that the textbooks in the 1949 study were found to be "distressingly inadequate, inappropriate and even damaging to intergroup relations" (p. 1). Just a few years later, Morton Sobel (1954) focused his review to fifteen seventh grade social studies texts. He concluded that in terms of how they dealt with nationality, social class, race and religion, some stereotypes of minorities persisted but that they were not necessarily derogatory. Comparing forty-eight textbooks used during the 1950s and early 1960s, Lloyd Marcus (1961) concluded that the treatment of African Americans and other minorities had made some uneven gains since 1949.

In 1969, James Banks reviewed thirty-six history textbooks used in fourth through eighth grades for their treatment of race relations and of African Americans. Using a thematic analysis of eleven categories, including discrimination and achievement, he also compared the frequency of themes in six textbooks from 1964 and 1968. Banks found that many authors failed to explain prejudice and discrimination and rarely depicted violence. He also found that the treatment of African Americans had significantly improved since 1964, and that 1968 texts relied less on stereotypes (Banks, 1969).

Using the criteria from Marcus' 1961 study, Michael Kane (1970) examined forty-five social studies textbooks published in the 1960s. Although he also noted some improvement, he discovered that Asians, Chicanos, Puerto Ricans, and Native Americans received very uneven treatment. In a yearlong study conducted by the Dallas chapter of the American Jewish Committee, the group examined fifth and eighth grade level history textbooks on the official adoption list for Texas in 1975. This group of educators and laypersons recognized that progress has been made in removing racial bias. However, they still found glaring examples of ethnocentrism, stereotyping and negative characterizations of African Americans, Chicanos, and Native Americans (Simms, 1975).

In her study of textbook treatment of U.S. history five years later, Frances Fitzgerald (1980) found that in terms of minorities, the coverage represented a compromise between diverse constituents and interest groups. That same year, Jesus Garcia (1980) examined twenty U.S. history texts published in the 1970s had found that although authors used a variety of themes when chronicling the historical role of Native Americans, some key issues such as treaty rights and land policy were covered only superficially.

Upon examining six secondary level U.S. history textbooks published in the 1970s, Nathan Glazar and Reed Ueda (Glazar & Ueda, 1983) found that African Americans and Native Americans received more thorough treatment than did Hispanics and Asian Americans. Then, in an attempt to identify changes in the treatment of African Americans over time, Garcia and Goebel (1985) compared a group of five textbooks written between

1956 and 1975 with another group of ten textbooks written in the 1980s. They found that the breadth of coverage had increased beyond slavery, Reconstruction, and the Civil Rights Movement to include such topics as Black churches and organizations. However, the depth of coverage on these and other topics still remained superficial.

Clearly, these studies and others show that there has been some discernible increase in the quantity and diversity of descriptions found in history textbooks in reference to minorities and women. There has not been, however, according to Garcia (1993) as significant a gain in the quality of these increasingly diverse representations. Based on the studies he has reviewed, Garcia also asserts that, " . . . the treatment of minorities in textbooks has not improved dramatically in the social sciences . . . Moreover, there is little or no content suggesting a global connection to cultural diversity . . . Thus readers are provided with a limited view of multiculturalism" (Garcia, 1993, p. 7).

A review of textbook representations of Latinos should include recognition of the obvious and ever-present global connections U. S. Hispanics have to Latin America. In that context, Cook (1985) noted that like the mass media, social studies textbooks present "an incomplete or biased portrait of the countries making up Latin America" (p. 1). Gallup polls indicated that it is a region about which Americans were poorly informed and that while news programs focus on spectacular events like hurricanes, coups, and sometimes U.S. foreign policy there, "It is rare to find stories on the arts, humanities, or culture of Latin America" (Glab, 1981, p. 69).

In a survey of ten high school texts, Fleming (1982) noted that little recognition was given to cultural characteristics of Latin American nations. Their histories were presented primarily in the context of U.S. foreign policy, their views were rarely considered and negative stereotypes of Latin America and its citizens were created or reinforced.

From another contextual perspective, Salazar (1991) examined eleven textbooks on the very history of American education and another seven textbooks on Western educational history. The earliest text was published in 1874, and the rest were published throughout every decade of the twentieth century up to 1988. None of the seven texts on western education, however, make any mention of Hispanic topics, people or contributions. Among the eleven American education texts, although these books ranged from four to six hundred pages, no more than two pages were devoted to Hispanics.

Yet, Salazar noted that the first functioning university in the Americas, established in Mexico by 1553, helped set the pattern for universities that followed throughout the region. She further noted that the first school activities in what is now the United States occurred in provinces of New Spain such as Florida, California and Texas. Neither of these two historical facts were mentioned in these seventeen texts, nor were any of educational leaders who emerged and developments that occurred in the Southwest and throughout Hispanic America up to modern era.

Thus, the treatment of Latinos in U.S. history textbooks occurred within a general context of omission, distortion and underrepresentation regarding the wider Hispanic and Latin American history and heritage in the Americas.

In one of the earliest and most thorough studies focusing primarily on Hispanic coverage in textbooks, Jesus Garcia (1980) examined the assertion that overall, the literature indicates that since the early 1960s the depiction of Hispanics has become more balanced, realistic and sensitive to ethnic perspectives.

Garcia did both a quantitative and qualitative analysis of data on ten secondary U.S. history textbooks published in 1978 and 1979, using seven key questions about the quality of information regarding Hispanics, and then counting the number of sentences responding to each question. He also categorized and counted these sentences according to their focus on Mexican Americans, Puerto Ricans or Cuban Americans, as well as on Hispanics in general.

Garcia found that only limited descriptions of Hispanics were provided and that none of the texts adequately addressed the key questions asked. More attention was devoted to providing background on the problems than on the accomplishments of these three groups. Further compounding the problem-oriented focus of these texts was the shallow and distorted portrayal of Mexican Americans and Puerto Ricans.

While confining much discussion to such topics as unemployment, drugs, violence or even prejudice, Garcia found that textbooks omit serious discussion of other pivotal topics such as the Mexican American role in the development of the Southwest or the issues underlying U.S.-Puerto Rican relations.

In a 1986 report based on the analysis of thirty-one history textbooks, five historians working for the People for the American Way concluded that "Overall the treatment of Hispanics . . . perpetuates their invisible roles in building the nation. Hispanics . . . have long been ignored or casually mentioned in conventional U.S. history textbooks" (de Varona, 1989, p. 3).

Linda K. Salvucci (1991) scrutinized ten textbooks approved for use in the state of Texas between 1986 and 1992. Five texts covered pre-Civil War U.S. history at the eighth grade, and the other five were used in the post-Civil War high school history course. Looking closely at how each text dealt with Mexico, Mexicans and Mexican Americans during key eras and events, Salvucci found that the texts presented very mixed images. While some texts treated a few events and eras adequately, no one textbook or series by the same publisher sustained its occasionally successful treatment of the three topics across time. Mexican and Mexican American perspectives were almost never elaborated, even for pivotal events such as the Mexican American War. Things Mexican were only characterized as problems for the United States, and some of the old nineteenth century racial stereotypes still persisted.

Published that same year was a study by Sleeter and Grant (1991)who examined fourteen social studies textbooks used at the elementary level and published from 1980 to 1986. They found that Hispanics are featured in three percent or less of the pictures in nine books, and in eight percent of pictures in three books. In the narrative itself, Hispanics, mainly Mexican Americans, were mentioned only briefly and incidentally, and then mostly in discussions of early colonization, settlement of the Southwest, and the Mexican American War. Mexican perspectives were not presented with clarity and authority, as were American views. Neither was there any analysis of the socioeconomic nor the cultural factors that fostered the conflict between both nations. In some texts, Hispanics appeared in more recent times only as "illegal aliens" living in urban areas.

Focusing on two fifth grade textbooks published in 1988 and 1991, and approved for adoption in Texas schools, Arries (1994) also discovered considerable omissions, distortions and stereotyping in the coverage of Mexican Americans and Mexicans. Both the text and illustrations presented a biased view of four key events: the Alamo battle, the War for Texas Independence, the War with Mexico, and the Civil Rights Movement.

Beyond the elementary and secondary levels, even post-secondary textbooks provided a less than adequate coverage of Hispanics. In her review of four college-level American history textbooks published in 1984 and 1985, Vicki L. Ruiz (1987) found that with the exception of one text, the textbooks mentioned Hispanics, particularly Mexican Americans and Puerto Ricans, the two largest groups, only in passing. A 919-page text had but a single page dealing with Hispanics! Another devoted two paragraphs out of a total of 867 pages, and the third contained three paragraphs in a book that was 1,343 pages long.

It is clear from the above overview that at every level of schooling from elementary through college, American history textbooks generally have done little justice to the topic of Hispanics in terms of the quantity and the quality of coverage.

That considerable progress has been made from the first half of the twentieth century is worth noting. However, more research in this area of textbook evaluation needs to be done on texts published during the 1990s and beyond in order to better determine to what extent this progress has continued. Moreover, this research could also indicate where authors and publishers currently are in this regard and where they need to go in order to significantly improve the treatment of Latinos in U.S. history textbooks.

TEACHERS' ROLE AND INFLUENCING FACTORS

Several studies have documented the important role history teachers play in selecting content, using instructional methods, and utilizing educational materials including textbooks, maps, and audiovisuals. These and other investigations have also identified some of the factors which influence history teachers' curricular and instructional decisions, including structural conditions in the school, community and student characteristics, as well as their own beliefs, values, social class, knowledge, and training.

In terms of content choice, a 1989–90 survey conducted by the National Center for History in the Schools at UCLA found that high school U.S. history teachers spend more classroom time teaching about the twentieth century than the earlier history of the nation. The main teaching tool for most of the four hundred eighty-one teachers was a survey textbook, and few were frequent users of such materials as biographies, documents or literature of the period (Thomas, 1992).

Among the structural conditions, there were a variety of factors that have been found to limit and direct how and what history teachers instruct. The sheer teaching load and multiple preparations meant that there was less time for teachers to plan and grade more challenging lessons given to students (Morrissett, 1981; Shaver, et al., 1978). There was also a variety of structural constraints that affected social studies teachers, such as ineffectual leadership, lack of materials, and limited development opportunities (Little, 1989).

Many teachers perceived that the community prefers conservative approaches to teaching which emphasize content transmission (Fawcet & Hawke, 1982; Jarolimek, 1981). Some teachers also perceived that students lacked interest in social studies (Eslinger & Superka, 1982), and even used this as a rationale for covering the basics and not engaging students in more complex inquiry activities (McKee, 1988; Stake, et al., 1978).

Considering the influence of their beliefs and background, history teachers were not just "passive transmitters of knowledge" (Elbaz, 1981, p. 43). They brought their own individual attitudes and experiences and applied these in making decisions about what content they cover in the classroom (Ben-Peretz, 1990).

In a more recent study, Romanowski (1997) found that beliefs, life experiences, family and social class, school climate, community, students, and testing all exerted a significant impact on history teachers' curriculum decisions. In an earlier study, Romanowski (1995) had investigated how U.S. history teachers used their textbooks and the factors that influenced their use of the textbook. He found that "textbook knowledge does not pass perfectly from text to student" (p. 26); rather it is the manner in which the teacher manages the textbook and other materials that determine what students ultimately learn.

His four major findings were that: 1) teachers view the textbook as a starting point to be supplemented with additional sources; 2) teachers believe it is important to raise democratic ideals through the teaching of history, including such values as justice, equality, freedom, civil rights, and antiracism; 3) teachers indicated that the beliefs of students and the community influenced their approach to the textbook, and teaching U.S. history; and 4) there was a wide range of teachers' abilities to discuss and critique the biases and omissions of the textbook (Romanowski, 1995).

Another factor that was influencing U.S. history teachers in their curricular choices and approaches was the growing diversity of the student body, of their communities, and American society at large. The push for including women and minorities was being increasingly reflected in textbooks, supplementary materials, relevant readings, and instructional activities.

MULTICULTURAL EDUCATION: RATIONALES AND APPROACHES

One very powerful motivation driving the multicultural movement is the fact that the mainstream curriculum has been, and despite some recent changes, largely continues to be Anglocentric, Eurocentric, patriarchal, and class biased (Banks, 1999; Levine, 1996; Nieto, 1992; Spring, 1997).

Another factor energizing multicultural education, as documented in a previous section, is that textbooks have a long history of marginalizing racial and ethnic minorities, as they do women, and continue to misrepresent or underrepresent them in their narratives until quite recently (Banks, 1969; Fitzgerald, 1980; Garcia, 1980, 1993; Garcia & Goebel, 1985; Glazer & Ueda, 1983; Kane, 1970; Marcus, 1961; Simms, 1975; Sobol, 1954).

Contributing to the controversy over multicultural education is its multiple meanings in practice and in the professional literature itself. Yet there is a consensus developing among scholars about what the major goals of multicultural education are. Banks (1999) identifies two of them:

1. to increase educational equality for both gender groups, for students from diverse ethnic and cultural groups, and for exceptional students. (p. 22)
2. to help all students . . . develop the knowledge, skills and attitudes they will need to survive and function effectively in a future U.S. society in which one out of every three people will be a person of color. (p. 23)

Other goals identified by Banks include:

3. to help individuals gain greater self-understanding by viewing themselves from the perspectives of other cultures. (p. 2)
4. to provide students with cultural and ethnic alternatives so as to counter the negative effects an Anglocentric curriculum has on many students of color. (p. 2)
5. to reduce the pain and discrimination that members of some ethnic and racial groups experience because of their unique racial, physical, and cultural characteristics. (p. 3)

Many critics also fail to recognize certain assumptions made by multicultural scholars and practitioners such as the facts that

- Race, culture, ethnicity and social class are salient parts of U.S. society
- Ethnic and cultural diversity enriches the nation and increases opportunities for diversifying problem solving approaches.
  (Banks, 1999)

Louis Harris and Associates conducted a national survey of Hispanic, African American and White students from rural, suburban and urban areas. These diverse students responded to several questions related to multicultural education: the availability of these courses, their interest in taking them, their opinions on the emphasis their schools placed on them, and their evaluations of how well their teachers taught about tolerance (Lietman, Binns, & Steinberg, 1996).

One of the most significant findings was that just over 70% of students nationwide expressed an interest in learning more about cultural events that people celebrate in different parts of the world. Less than half (45%) students responded that they were satisfied with the emphasis their schools placed on teaching multiculturalism. Yet, of the nearly 40% who were dissatisfied, most would prefer their schools to place more, rather than less, emphasis on multicultural education.

In a previous survey on violence and social tensions, students had indicated that social relations among students from different racial, ethnic and economic backgrounds are improved when teachers do a good job of teaching tolerance. When asked to rate teachers on how well they are teaching tolerance in this subsequent survey, less than half the students (44%) said their teachers did an average job. About one-fourth of the students felt their teachers did well, but almost one-fifth said teachers did a poor job of teaching tolerance (Lietman, et al., 1996).

These and other findings, according to the project directors, provide an important and encouraging message to educators about three key aspects that must be considered:

1.   the high level of student interest in multicultural programs,
2.   the need to expand these programs and,
3.   the likely benefit to both students and teachers if multiculturalism is given greater attention in the schools. (Ibid)

As a relatively new field of theory and practice, multicultural education does require more research, experimentation, and ultimately, greater refinement. Yet, it is a sound and worthy practice that requires dedication and often courage just to establish and maintain, let alone expand and improve.

Although findings from empirical research on the effects of multicultural education are relatively sparse, there are encouraging discoveries from those that do exist:

- Negative racial and ethnic attitudes toward others can be changed through deliberate intervention, but the process is long range.
- Establishing a closer fit between teaching styles and culturally different learning styles has positive social and academic consequences.
- Alternative instructional means can be used to achieve common outcome expectations without compromising the educational standards and quality of anyone.

- Some instructional techniques are more effective than others for some members of ethnic and cultural groups.
- Instructional initiatives that work well for groups of color generally benefit Anglo students, too. However, the converse is not true. Educational interventions that are successful with Anglo students often have negative consequences for culturally different students.
- The procedures of teaching and learning are important targets of intervention for multicultural change. They are as significant as the content and substance of teaching, if not more so.
- Culturally sensitive teaching techniques that work well with diverse students appear to be effective across age, gender, school settings, and subjects (Gay, 1994).

PERSONAL RESEARCH ON RELEVANT TOPICS

Prior to these research efforts which comprise this investigation, several studies I conducted provided relevant background information on two topics: 1) creation and content of the world history TEKS curriculum standards, and 2) the impact Anglocentric curriculum and mass media have on Latino students.

Creation and Content of World History TEKS

Doing research for the paper, *Missing pages from the human story: World history according to TEKS,* gave me the opportunity to investigate the content of the Texas Essential Knowledge and Skills curriculum standards for world history, as well as the process by which these and other social studies standards were written and established (Noboa, 1998).

The world history course is briefly described thus in the TEKS:

> World History Studies is the only course that offers students an overview of all of human history . . . [it is] the only course that allows students the opportunity to examine major ideas and themes over time and over space. The major emphasis is on the study of significant people, events, and ideas from the earliest time to the present . . . By attempting to explain the past, world history helps students to understand the present, thus enabling them to make informed decisions and to develop an appreciation of their own heritage (TEA, 1996).

Founded on the assumption that global influences and challenges are perhaps greater now than ever before for our state and nation, the research was motivated by the fundamental question: *To what extent are the TEKS for world history preparing students to "make informed decisions" about future global challenges?*

More specifically, the research was guided by the following specific question: *To what extent does the TEKS for world history present an accurate, inclusive and objective overview of "significant people, events, and ideas from the earliest time to the present?"*

Answering that question required considerable detailed review of the contents of the TEKS world history curriculum standards, and it did generate much useful and relevant data. But before discussing these findings about the content, however, we will briefly review some vital information about the curriculum development process that this research also uncovered.

The creation of the TEKS involved a three year process of writing drafts, holding hearings and revising rewrites profoundly influenced by political, religious and ideological considerations (Bernal, 1997; Offutt, 1997; TEA, 1997a; TEA, 1997b).

All curricular areas including English, math, science, technology, fine arts, foreign languages and social studies were rewritten. It was the first major curriculum revision in over ten years for the Texas Education Agency and involved many Texas citizens with 127 serving in review panels, 350 in writing teams, and no less than 18,000 providing oral or written testimony

As stated above in the Introduction, for every TEKS content area, a diverse team of teachers, parents, college faculty, curriculum specialists and business people was selected to produce the written standards. The social studies writing team consisted of thirty-five members with twenty-one Euroamericans, nine Hispanics, four African Americans and one American Indian. Seventeen of them were teachers while the rest included six social studies coordinators, five instructional administrators, four university academics, two parents and one business person (TEA, 1997b).

Although there clearly was an effort by TEA to include racial and occupational diversity in this social studies writing team, it would have been difficult to ascertain the political or ideological perspectives of participants within this writing team, and how these perspectives influenced the writing process.

However difficult it was to ascertain certain aspects of this process, the contents of the TEKS itself, whose review comprised the major focus of the study, were more clearly open and evident than the process that engendered them. The TEKS consists of a collection of Knowledge and Skills Areas (KSA), each with statements specifying a topical area of knowledge or skills to be mastered by the student. Each KSA includes stated expectations by which to evaluate students' proficiency in that topical area.

In the TEKS for world history, there are a total of twenty-seven KSAs, including three in social studies skills, four in culture, and ten in history proper. Within those ten areas of history, four deal with specific cultures and civilizations, and these four were the first set of KSAs whose content was reviewed for the purpose of the research.

These four KSAs, KSA #3 through #6, encompassed the actual scope of the strictly historical segment of the course. Of these four areas, three focused strictly on Europe, and the fourth one, literally lumped together all the other civilizations in human history. The major topics covered for each KSA are:

#3 The Western Roman Empire and early Western Europe
#4 The European Renaissance & the Reformation
#5 The European Expansion
#6 Civilizations of Asia, Sub-Saharan Africa, Mesoamerica, and Andean South America (TEA, 1997b, p. C-13).

Whereas a natural Eurocentric focus and greater attention to Europe than other continents is understandable given that ours is essentially a Western society with European foundations, however, the obvious relegation of all other civilizations to a single KSA is indefensible. Given that students are exposed to European and/or Western ideas, culture, literature, achievements, and civilizations throughout the curriculum in every subject area, especially in social studies, this aspect of the world history TEKS does not expose students enough to nonwestern civilizations about which they know relatively little or nothing. In addition to the sheer misbalance of coverage, there are some important civilizations, including Mesopotamia, Ancient Egypt, and Islamic civilization, which cannot be covered adequately, if at all, given the description of KSA #6. Students stand to lose much valuable world history given that the first two mentioned above were among the four pristine cradles of civilization in the Old World, and that the third one has a historical relationship with the West and is becoming more relevant to global concerns.

This Eurocentric focus to the exclusion of other vital areas of world history knowledge is also evident in several other KSAs, most notably in the KSA #8 which deals with the concept of *Revolutions* and reads thus: "The student understands causes and effects of major political revolutions since the 17th century."

The student is expected to:

(A) identify causes and evaluate effects of major political revolutions
     since the 17th century, including the English, American, French,
     and Russian revolutions;

(B) summarize the ideas from the English, American, French, and
     Russian revolutions . . .

(C) evaluate how the American Revolution differed from the French
     and Russian revolutions . . . and

(D) summarize the significant events related to the spread and fall of
     communism, including worldwide political and economic effects
     (TEA, 1997b, p. C-14).

Whereas the four revolutions cited are very significant and worthy of study,
they were all Western revolutions, again showing an obvious Eurocentric
bias; but even more importantly, several pivotal revolutions, all occurring
in the Third World within the last century, are excluded.

Not mentioned by name are the Chinese, Cuban, and Vietnamese revolutions, all socialist, but also nationalist struggles against what was perceived as imperialist domination by Western powers. Although these could
conceivably be covered under the description of section D, their very exclusion by name raises suspicions about the political agendas at work.

Also missing are the African and Latin American revolutions for
national liberation, again against European powers, revolutions that have
shaped the history of these two huge landmasses for decades, if not centuries. Also most notably excluded are both Mexican revolutions, one for
national liberation in the nineteenth and the other for socioeconomic
reforms in the twentieth century.

Absent as well is the Indian Revolution, also against a European
empire, but most notably the only deliberately nonviolent revolution for
national liberation in recent history. Thus, key moral and historical lessons
from Mohatmas Ghandi and other liberators and movements are denied to
Texas students.

Given the influence these Third World revolutions have had on world
history, politics, and culture, as well as their undeniable and direct impact on
our own history (consider the Cuban, Mexican and Vietnamese revolutions),
it is inexcusable to exclude them from any course in world history. The message communicated to students, then, is that the causes, effects and ideas of
these Third World leaders and revolutions are not significant enough to be
mentioned or seriously studied in the context of world history.

These were only some of the discoveries this study made about the contents of the world history TEKS, a foundational curricular document used as

a basis for textbooks, teaching and teacher training. When all the findings are considered, revealing obvious biases, exclusions, and subsequent distortions of world history, this study arrived at the following conclusions:

1. TEKS World History Studies is clearly Eurocentric in its approach to world history. The contributions and achievements of many significant non-European civilizations are either missing or minimized.
2. Texas students will have no basis for knowing or understanding the most globally significant revolutions that occurred in the Third World during the last two centuries, including those in our own hemisphere.
3. Texas students will not comprehend the rationale underlying Third World resistance to European imperialism nor the geopolitical foundations for many of the global issues that still create destructive tensions today, some of which led up to the September 11 attacks.
4. Students will gain no knowledge of how the U.S. and other Western empires supported dictatorships, toppled democratic governments, and exploited the labor, resources and markets of Third World nations.
5. Students in Texas, but especially Mexican American students, who represent over one-third of our public school population, would have no opportunity outside of the brief Mesoamerican coverage, to learn anything about Mexico in the context of world history, despite Mexico's direct relevance to Texas and to American history. This parallels the decades of underrepresentation and misrepresentation Mexico and Mexican Americans have received in the entire history curriculum.

(Noboa, 1998).

Thus, returning to the specific question that guided this content analysis research effort: *To what extent does the TEKS for world history present an accurate, inclusive and objective overview of "significant people, events, and ideas from the earliest time to the present?"* The answer, regrettably, is "to a very limited extent."

Anglocentric Curriculum and Mass Media

The other study, which served as a contextual antecedent to those comprising this investigation, focused on the effect Anglocentric curricula and mass media have on Latino students. Entitled, *Growing up Latino in Anglocentric schools: The impact of school and media curricula,* the inquiry was guided by two related research questions. The first question, responded to through a review of the relevant literature in the sub-discipline of Educational Anthropology, asks:

> *How and to what extent are Latino students' attitudes towards ethnic identity and their responses towards schooling impacted by a predominantly Eurocentric or Anglocentric school curriculum?*

The second question guiding this inquiry was based on the recognition that there is a "societal curriculum," which in concert with the "school curriculum" exerts an undeniable influence on Latino students, as it does on all students (Cortés, 1997). Thus, in order to provide a wider context from which to consider the primary question, a secondary question was also formulated:

> *What kinds of images and messages about Latinos are Latino students, and the general American public, being exposed to through English language television and major films?*

These two questions, though seemingly distinct and involving different disciplines, are interrelated in significant ways. Most notably, the societal curriculum as expressed in the most powerful media of television and films provides the cultural and informational context in which schooling takes place for all students. If the media messages provide negative images and stereotypes of Latinos, schools become the only other institutional source, outside the home and the community, which can either support or contradict the misinformation Latino students receive about themselves as a group.

The bulk of literature reviewed in this inquiry was focused on the primary question while fewer sources, mainly from the growing literature on Latino media studies, yielded information for the secondary question. Nevertheless, this secondary question will help frame the school experience of Latinos in the wider context of the most powerful mass media they consume outside of school. So we will begin there.

It is not enough to consider the "home" or "community" culture when discussing the transcultural implications of schooling for Latino students. Like all others, Latino students are media consumers of music, film, magazines, and television, and as such are profoundly influenced by this mass media in multiple ways. One of those ways is how they view and think about diversity (Cortés, 2000).

Whatever that media tells them about who they are, and whatever aspects of that media culture they have internalized, Latino students bring to school along with their home language and culture.

In a national survey conducted in March, 1998, Children Now asked questions about television viewing by children of four ethnoracial groups, African Americans, Euroamericans, Asians and Latinos, especially as it related to perceptions of race and class broadcast on TV (Children Now, 1998). The four groups were: Several findings regarding television viewing in connection with race in general and Latinos specifically, are interesting and relevant, especially the last listed here:

- Children of all races watch a great deal of television including a wide variety of different kinds of programs.
- 71% of White Children see people of their race 'very often' on television compared to 42% of African American children, 22% of Latino children and 16% of Asian children.
- Across all races, children are more likely to associate positive characteristics with White characters and negative characteristics with minority characters.
- Children have great faith in media's power and its potential. Over 80% of children of every race believe that media can teach children "that people of their race are important."
- All races agree that Latinos are the most likely to be portrayed negatively on entertainment programs (Ibid).

A 1997 study by the National Council of La Raza (NCLR), one of the premier and largest national Latino civil rights organizations, arrived at the following two conclusions: "Hispanics are almost invisible in both the entertainment and mass media." and "When Hispanics do appear, they are consistently and uniformly portrayed more negatively than other race and ethnic groups." (National Council of La Raza, 1997).

The "Watching America" study on thirty years of television (from 1955 to 1986) by the Center for Media and Public Affairs revealed much about Hispanic representation on TV:

- Hispanics have remained at only about 2%, going from bad in 1950s at 3%, to even worse in the late 1980s to a mere 1%.
- During 1955—86 period: 11% of White characters were criminals, only 7% of Black characters were, but 22% of Latino characters were thus portrayed.

- In fact, "despite being outnumbered three to one, Hispanic characters have committed more violent crimes than Blacks on television" (NCLR, 1997).

Another NCLR study of fictional programming for the 1992–93 TV season revealed that

- Black representation nearly tripled from 6% in 1955->86 to 17% in 1992->93
- Hispanic representation dropped from 2% to 1% (Thus by 1992–93, there were seventeen Black TV characters for every one Latino)
- Latinos were twice as likely as Whites and three times as likely as Blacks to be portrayed in negative roles (Latinos=18%; Whites=8%, and Blacks=6%) (Ibid)

Some of the most prevalent media stereotypes about Latinos as TV characters were identified through several studies by NCLR. Too often Latinos are portrayed as

- having low SES, being very poor, and/or lazy
- failures, or characters who experience lack of success
- people who do not have to be taken seriously
- untrustworthy, "deceivers or tricksters" (Ibid)

The impact this media has on Latino students could not be ignored, although it is probably difficult to measure without further study precisely how these media distortions impact the students' sense of self-esteem, ethnic identity, and personal motivation. However, given the well documented misrepresentation of Latinos in the most powerful mass medium, the primary question guiding this inquiry gains even more importance, and it becomes more imperative to determine what happens to Latinos students' self concept and interest in schooling when the curriculum excludes them or provides only token attention. Again, the question is:

> How and to what extent are Latino students' attitudes towards ethnic identity and their responses towards schooling impacted by a predominantly Eurocentric or Anglocentric school curriculum?

Based on extensive fieldwork in specific schools and communities educational anthropologists have made several relevant observations and arrived at significant conclusions pertinent to this question.

After collecting ethnographic data from 1986–1989 in a Los Angeles high school with an 80% Latino student population and a predominantly Anglo teaching staff, Patthey-Chavez made some revealing discoveries about the cultural clashes occurring at that school, " . . . the high school is an arena in which the boundary between Latino and Anglo culture is being negotiated, with "minority" and "majority" in conflict over the extent to which their versions of a cultural identity are to be reproduced in the American educational system" (Patthey-Chavez, 1993, p. 33).

With the exception of one Cinco de Mayo celebration organized by a Chicano counselor, all the extracurricular activities in the school had, according to Patthey-Chavez, a "distinct American flavor." Trophies were proudly displayed for track and football, but the school did not focus resources on their soccer team and never "got its soccer coaching together," despite the fact that the team had some virtuoso players, and was of high interest to Latino students (Ibid, p. 51).

Patthey-Chavez also observed that the school personnel operated in a "semiotic bubble" that they worked hard to maintain every day. This bubble kept them separated and shielded from the predominantly Latino community surrounding the high school. She describes teachers as having a singular cultural mission: "to preserve and inculcate an American identity through the practices of an all-American high school." When the faculty's Americanization agenda conflicted too greatly with that of its students, the students would either "pull back in silence, refuse to ratify it, or even push it out through disruptive behavior" (Ibid, p. 54).

This reliance on mainstreaming socialization practices was likely to cause, according to Patthey-Chavez, increased conflict with students who "simply accepted that their teachers came from a different universe." (p. 54) As a result students become more apathetic towards both academic and extracurricular activities of the school.

Thus, in the face of an Anglo-Americanizing cultural mission, many Latino students either withdrew or acted out, neither response being constructive nor conducive to academic achievement. The administration and teachers evidently were not aware of or sensitive to the source of the problem; or perhaps did not have the knowledge and skills to help Latino students cope successfully with these cultural contradictions and discontinuities.

Margaret Gibson also discussed how many Latino students resist school authority as a way of maintaining their ethnic identity in response to the acculturation pressures within the schools:

> Schools today, as in the past, convey to minority youngsters that to be successful in school and to be "true Americans" they must give up their minority identities . . . The point I which to emphasize is . . . the perception on the part of many minority children that school learning is associated with acculturation and, in turn, that acquisition of cultural competencies in the ways of the majority group means, ultimately, the loss of their distinctive ethnic and cultural identities. Hence, to maintain their identity many minority youngsters believe that they must resist school authority (Gibson, 1989, p. 130–1).

However, Gibson discovered as well that some Latino and minority students did achieve within the academic environment by pursuing the bilingual-bicultural strategy of what she labels "acculturation without assimilation."

> By way of contrast, at least some of the minority students who do well in school, both immigrant and nonimmigrant, pursue a strategy that I have labeled *acculturation without assimilation*. They see acquisition of skills in the majority-group language and culture in an *additive* rather than a *subtractive* fashion, leading not to a rejection of their minority-group identity but to a successful participation in both mainstream and minority worlds (Ibid, p. 131).

In the context of a discussion about achievement motivation among Hispanic immigrant students, Suarez-Orozco also discusses assimilative pressures and critiques some theoretical models of cultural discontinuity used to explain school failure among Latinos:

> . . . in the case of the Hispanic American it has been argued simplistically that a somehow asphyxiating cultural matrix orienting individuals heavily to the family is responsible for crippling achievement motivation. . . . Such reasoning typically leads to variants of an 'assimilative' genre, where cultural diversities are eventually truncated. Rodriquez' tale is one such version (Rodriquez, 1982). Achievement in his case was only possible at the expense of turning away from his family and his community. The price of his achievement was a severe sense of alienation from his group . . . (Suarez-Orozco, 1989, p. 113).

Like Gibson, Suarez-Orozco also observed that some Latino students, more specifically Central American youth, had found ways to succeed in academics while maintaining a firm ethnic identity in the context of family and community:

> . . . the kind of radical acculturation advocated by Richard Rodriquez and others as required for motivation and school success is not the only alternative. Some Central American youth, among whom I worked, became very successful in the Anglo-American idiom without having to give up their ethnic identity. . . . On the contrary, their dreams and deeds were embedded in a socio-cultural matrix of family and community cooperation, affiliation and mutual nurturance (Ibid, p. 114).

While the very existence of some Latino students who develop a bicultural and bilingual strategy for success is encouraging, the fact remains that given the Anglocentric pressures and curriculum, the vast majority of them have difficulty making this strategy work for them. The high drop out rates of Latinos students, the relatively few who complete a college education, and the cultural alienation of many of those who do achieve academically, are all indicators of the underlying cultural discontinuities between educational institutions and Latino students.

The fact that the mass media also does a dismal job of representing Latinos objectively or realistically, if at all, creates an overall cultural climate that places an undue burden on the Latino families and communities to provide historical and cultural context for their children and youth. Given the social and economic challenges already facing these communities and families, few resources are left to deal with anything but issues of survival, safety, and security. Therefore, few Latino students are able to access the resources necessary to gain, develop and maintain a healthy and productive ethnic self-concept.

If the mass media consistently portrays Latinos rarely or negatively, then one of the few arenas for Latino students to obtain objective, authentic, detailed information about who they are as a people is in school. Unfortunately, most schools are probably not up to this task.

The methods employed in both of these studies, namely content analyses and targeted literature reviews, provided good opportunities for this researcher to refine those approaches that would later be used in this investigation. These studies not only helped provide this researcher with a wider environmental context for understanding the role of the mass media and the school curriculum in the representation of Latinos; they also provided a deeper sociological understanding as to why it is important for public educators to become more multicultural in their practice, and to pay increased attention to what they teach students about the largest minority group in America today.

Chapter Two
Relevant Theory and Validity

APPLICABLE AND RELEVANT THEORY

There are two theoretical foundations for understanding the overall issues and topics explored through this investigation. One is the collection of ideas and concepts that define multicultural education, some of which were described above in previous chapters.

The other relevant theoretical foundation is critical race theory, specifically those premises that address the distinctions that characterize the varied experiences of different ethnic and racial groups in America. Critical race theory holds that although there are some commonalities of experience and struggle between, for example, African Americans and Latinos in America, each group has a distinct history and separate set of concerns vis-à-vis the Anglo power structure.

Multicultural Education

Beginning with the concepts of multicultural education, the results or findings of this investigation could be interpreted in the context of how, and to what extent, the teaching of U.S. history in Texas has been influenced by and has responded to the presence of Latinos and other minorities in the student body and the body politic of the state.

One very useful concept, expressed by one of the founders of the multicultural education movement, James A. Banks, is that of the four approaches to curriculum transformation used by educators in response to the realities of growing cultural diversity in the schools.

These four approaches are conceived by Banks as actually being four levels, each one more effective than the last, with the fourth representing the highest and most transformative approach to integrating cultural content into the school or university curriculum:

1. Contributions Approach
   Focuses on heroes, holidays, and discrete cultural elements
2. Additive Approach
   Content, concepts, themes, and perspectives are added to the
   curriculum without changing its structure.
3. Transformation Approach
   The structure of the curriculum is changed to enable students to
   view concepts, issues, events, and themes from the perspective of
   diverse ethnic and cultural groups.
4. Social Action Approach
   Students make decisions on important social issues and take
   actions to help solve them.

                                                    (Banks, 1999, p. 31).

This concept of different levels of approaches to cultural content integration could be quite useful to this investigation given that the content analyses of the TEKS, the textbooks, the textbook testimonies, and the teachers'
self-described classroom practices could each be characterized as representing one approach, or a combination of these. My intent is to note at which
of the four levels instruction is being imparted by textbooks, curriculum
guidelines and classroom teaching.

   This will help provide a basis for further analyses and comparisons
across each of these key aspects of the U.S. history curriculum. For example, the data could reveal that although teachers may be inclined to use a
Transformation Approach, the TEKS guidelines or the textbooks could be
written using an Additive or a Contributions Approach.

   Several other concepts emerging from multicultural education are relevant to this investigation. This begins with its theoretical aspects, since
Sleeter and Grant point out that multicultural education more than other
approaches, has experienced a mixing of theory and ideology, a combination that can often cause confusion (Sleeter and Grant, 1994).

   Nevertheless, these authors clearly define ideology simply as "what
ought to be" and contrast that with theory, defined as "why things are as
they are, and under what conditions things change in the desired direction"
(ibid, p. 176). Using as an example the concept of cultural pluralism, one of
the two main components of multicultural education, Sleeter and Grant
demonstrate how it is both an ideological component as well as a theoretical concept.

   In its ideological function, cultural pluralism is a belief that has been
defined in a variety of ways but that has distinctive elements, "Although

these definitions vary, all suggest that cultural pluralism includes the maintenance of diversity, a respect for differences, and the right to participate actively in all aspects of society without having to give up one's unique identity" (Ibid, p. 170).

As a theory, cultural pluralism is one which, according to Sleeter & Grant, supports the ideology of multicultural education. Basing their discussion on the work of William Newman (1973), they summarize four main theories related to this concept:

1. Assimilation: Over time the values and lifestyles of the minority group are replaced by those of the dominant group.
2. Amalgamation: The melting pot concept whereby all groups are combined and synthesized to become a distinct new group.
3. Classical Cultural Pluralism: Over time, minority groups persist in maintaining their values and lifestyles.
4. Modified Cultural Pluralism: Minority groups will assimilate into the dominant group, but the degree of assimilation will vary, and some will continue to retain unique cultural characteristics.
                                              (Sleeter & Grant, 1994, p. 176–80).

Considering each one, the authors explain that the first theory, Assimilation is obviously inaccurate, because distinct groups still exist and continue to differentiate themselves from the dominant group. Amalgamation has not occurred yet either, and the Classical Cultural Pluralism, though a better model than the first two, still does not account for the fact that considerable assimilation has and still does occur. Thus, they conclude that Newman's own Modified Cultural Pluralism model is the best of the four theories; it more accurately explaining the realities of minority-majority dynamics in this nation over time.

This is directly relevant to this investigation because it provides a convenient method of measuring and comparing how the curriculum, more specifically the guidelines, textbooks, and teaching of U.S. history, conforms to one or two of these models. It is significant to determine whether the overall teaching of U.S. history promotes assimilation, amalgamation or any of the two forms of cultural pluralism.

In addition to these theoretical multicultural models, also of relevance to this investigation are what Banks describes as the five "Dimensions of Multicultural Education." One dimension of particular significance to this effort is "Content Integration," defined thus: " . . . the extent to which teachers use examples, data, and information from a variety of cultures and groups to illustrate the key concepts, principles, generalizations, and theories in their subject area or discipline." (Banks, 1999, p. 14–15)

While characterizing this as a "narrow conception of multicultural education," and suggesting that too often multicultural education is viewed only as content integration, Banks does emphasize that this dimension has more relevance to social studies and language arts than to math or physics.

Thus, among the concepts we may use to analyze the data gathered from this investigation, will be "Content Integration," keeping in mind that this dimension by itself is not a full indicator of the extent to which students are being taught multiculturally.

Critical Race Theory

Other relevant theoretical concepts emerge from the field of critical race theory (CRT), which according to Delgado and Stefancic is a movement consisting of

> . . . a collection of activists and scholars interested in studying and transforming the relationship among race, racism, and power. The movement considers many of the same issues that conventional civil rights and ethnic studies discourses take up, but places them in a broader perspective that includes economics, history, context, group and self-interest, and even feelings and the unconscious.
> (Delgado & Stefancic, 2001, p. 2–3).

Although there are a considerable variety of beliefs and specific issues which the CRT movement encompasses, there are a several tenets or propositions upon which most CRT scholars agree. Among those agreements are

1. racism in our society is normal, not an aberration, therefore it is difficult to cure or address
2. our system of White-over-color ascendancy serves important material and psychic purposes
3. race and races are products of social thought and relations, and do not correspond to any significant biological or genetic realities
4. each race or ethnic group has its own origins and ever evolving history, with the dominant society creating shifting images and stereotypes of each group over time and circumstance
5. no person has a single, easily stated unitary identity, but rather has conflicting, overlapping identities, loyalties, and allegiances

6. because of their different histories and experiences with oppression, Black, Latino, Asian, Indian writers and thinkers may communicate to their White counterparts certain matters that they otherwise are unlikely to know (Ibid, 6–9).

The first two tenets above closely relate to this investigation because they could help explain the motivations and the mechanisms underlying the process of excluding Latinos and other minorities. Tenet #4 could also help explain the differential representation of Blacks versus Latinos in textbooks as well as in the mass media.

Another useful concept generating considerable controversy both within and outside the CRT movement, but which this researcher has observed and has confirmed in consultation with professional colleagues, is that of the *Black-White Binary*. It is an unstated paradigm or mindset that limits, frames and effectively distorts our discussion, understanding, and resolution of racial and ethnic issues. Delgado and Stefancic provide the following clear description of it:

> That paradigm, the black-white binary, effectively dictates that non-black minority groups must compare their treatment to that of African Americans to gain redress. The paradigm holds that one group, blacks, constitutes the prototypical minority group. 'Race' means quintessentially, African American. Other groups, such as Asians, Indians, and Latino/as, are minorities only in so far as their experience and treatment can be analogized to that of blacks (Ibid, p. 67–8).

The implications of this paradigm for the teaching of U.S. history are many. Suffice to point out for now, given that the experience of discrimination against Latinos is quite distinct from that of Blacks, especially when issues of language and land are concerned, an approach to history that defines oppression and the struggle against it only in Black terms would clearly ignore the Latino experience as being distinct, let alone significant enough to include in the curriculum. Civil rights and voting rights are examples of issues common to both Blacks and Latinos, but for Latinos, issues of language, culture, land, borders, citizenship, and immigration have much greater significance than they do for Blacks.

Latinos have suffered discrimination, for example, on the basis of speaking Spanish, a distinctly different language from English, and on the basis of citizenship, two issues which are not as relevant to most African Americans. The struggle for equality has taken various forms and strategies for each racial and ethnic group, and it would limit the scope of any history curriculum to include only those struggles that relate exclusively to the Black experience.

Other key concepts from critical race theory have significant relevance to educational issues in general, and specifically to our investigation. One such concept is that of the "master script." Critical race theory views the "official school curriculum" as an artifact designed to "maintain a White supremacist master script." (Ladson-Billings, 1999, p. 21)

Ladson-Billings quotes Swartz (1992) to provide a precise description of how "master scripting" functions:

> Master scripting silences multiple voices and perspectives, primarily legitimizing dominant, white, upper class, male voicings as the "standard" knowledge students need to know. All other accounts and perspectives are omitted from the master script unless they can be disempowered through misrepresentation (Swartz, 1992, p. 341).

In the context of our investigation, I will try to ascertain the extent to which data from the specific vehicles for knowledge transmission, namely the TEKS curriculum guidelines, the adopted textbooks, and classroom teaching, are "master scripted" to exclude or misrepresent minorities, most particularly Latinos.

In conclusion, both these sources of theory, multicultural education and critical race theory, were employed to help provide perspective as well as possible interpretations of the findings generated from this investigation. Used together, they provided me with a theoretical tool kit with which to better organize, understand and interpret the data gathered from these studies.

VALIDITY OF METHODS

There were two major sources of validity for all of these studies; they revolved around the specific procedures used to gather data for each study as well as the results of the data itself. The procedures affected validity in the sense that documented steps were taken, that the instruments used were sound and that they are described in sufficient detail so as to be replicated by another investigator.

In the case of TEKS, textbooks, and the textbook testimony, these documents are readily available, and if their content is approached and analyzed in a manner similar to what I utilized, I are confident that the resulting data will also be comparable if not identical to that which I generated.

For both the individual interviews and focus groups, the procedures and instruments were also, in my opinion, sound. Naturally, given the nature of the participation selection process, the resulting data might vary, especially in terms of participants' preferences, but I expect that overall the influence of certain structural factors such as standardized testing and the relative underrepresentation of Latinos from the classroom narrative, would be confirmed regardless of the specific participants.

The triangulation of data was the other major source of validity; it derived from the data itself and was related to the degree to which the data from content analyses of different key documents (TEKS, textbooks, course content checklists) demonstrate similar patterns of Latino and minority exclusion when compared to each other. The case for triangulation is also strengthened when the public testimony on textbooks as well as the views of U.S. history teachers in both the individual and focus group interviews, concur or agree on some fundamental issues regarding textbook representations and the influential role of TEKS, time restrictions, or standardized testing. Any other issues of validity specific to each method and area of study will be discussed in the corresponding chapters below.

The specific methods used in each of the four studies are also described in each of the following four chapters. As stated above, these four areas are TEKS, textbooks, teaching, and textbook testimony. Included within each description of methodology is a brief discussion of design, data collection, data analysis, and also participants when applicable. Each chapter also includes a complete presentation, discussion and analysis of the relevant data.

Chapter Three
TEKS Standards: Looking for Latinos

METHODS USED TO ANALYZE TEKS

The ultimate goal of this part of the study was to review and document the representation of Latinos in the TEKS for U.S. history (USHTEKS) at both the high school and middle school level. Another objective was to compare and contrast this representation with that of African Americans and American Indians. In Texas, the first part of U.S. history (before 1877) is taught in eighth grade and the second part is taught in the junior year of high school. I included both in this study.

For this investigation, I used content analysis based on a system of four levels, each labeled with a key word that identifies the significance and specificity of that level of representation and helps to make comparisons among the three-targeted groups.

Level 1: *Individual.* the specific name of an individual is mentioned, i.e., Martin Luther King, César Chávez, Sagajewea

Level 2: *Group.* indicates that the group is specified by name, i.e., Cherokee, Native Americans, Hispanic, Puerto Rican

Level 3: *Event.* an event, issue, or concept is included which implies presence of a group, i.e., Mexican American War, Emancipation Proclamation, Trail of Tears

Level 4: *Category.* the group is implied categorically by some generic term, i.e. "racial minority groups" or "immigrants"

In this context, Latino and Hispanic were used interchangeably and refer to persons of Spanish or Latin American descent. Terms such as Mexican American, Cuban, Puerto Rican, will be used to designate specific national origins whenever appropriate, and will be noted when mentioned in the TEKS.

The Texas Essential Knowledge and Skills (TEKS) consists of a collection of Knowledge and Skills Areas (KSA), each with statements specifying an area of knowledge or skills to be mastered by the student. Each KSA also includes stated expectations by which to evaluate students' proficiency in that area.

There are a total of thirty-two KSAs in the first part of U.S. history, and twenty-six in the second. The thirty-two KSAs for the first part of U.S. history, are distributed among eight specific thematic strands: history-9; geography-3; economics-3; government-4; citizenship-4; culture-4; science, technology and society-2; and social studies skills-3.

For the second part, the twenty-six KSAs are distributed thus: history-7; geography-4; economics-3; government-3; citizenship-2; culture-2; science, technology and society-2; and social studies skills-3. (TEA, 1997b, September).

Not every KSA was relevant to the specific goals of this inquiry; thus our discussion will be limited to those in which there is mention of any item associated with either of the three target groups.

Despite the critical tone of this inquiry, I recognize that overall the TEKS is a well-organized system of scope and sequence which provides an excellent framework for social studies. This review will focus on the content of the TEKS and only make reference to its structure when it serves to restrict or define the content.

By way of procedure, the entire content of U.S. History TEKS (USHTEKS) in both courses was reviewed and wherever there was mention of any individual, group, event, date or concept related to the Latino or Hispanic experience the entry was noted, counted and categorized. The same search was conducted for content related to African American and American Indian as well.

The count was then tallied for all four levels and three groups. The results for the TEKS for U.S. history, Part I, (through Reconstruction) are shown on Table 1, Part II is likewise shown on Table 2, and both parts are combined in Table 3. Please refer to Appendix A: Four Levels in TEKS to view all three tables on one page.

In addition to the count itself, each instance or item that mentioned any of the three groups at any level, was identified and discussed below.

DATA FROM THE TEKS

In the next section "U.S. History Through 1877," following immediately below, the content of the first course in U.S. history TEKS will be reviewed and analyzed wherever there is mention of any individual, group, event, date or concept related to the Latino experience in what is now the United States. The second course is similarly reviewed in the following section, "U.S. History Since 1877" and in the final section, "African Americans and American Indians," the representation of these two groups in both courses will be reviewed.

The data generated from these content analyses, is numerically summarized in Appendix A and is fully described below.

U.S. History Through 1877

Beginning with the nine KSAs focusing on history proper, in only two instances are items relevant to Latinos mentioned. The first occurs in KSA #8.2A History and relates to the fact that Hispanics in the Americas had their beginnings with the Spanish explorers, conquistadors, missionaries and settlers, although this is only implied by the wording: "The student is expected to: identify reasons for European exploration and colonization of North America" (TEA, 1997b, p. B-18).

Geographically, North America includes all of Mexico, and more importantly, there were regions in the southeast coast, in Florida, and especially in the Southwest, where Spaniards were the first to explore, map, and establish permanent settlements. Still, students are expected to identify the "reasons" for European exploration and colonization, which assumes they know who did it, when, where and why.

The second item occurs in #8.6D: "The student is expected to: explain the major issues and events of the Mexican War and their impact on the United States" (Ibid, p. B-20). These events and issues invariably involve Mexicans and among them those who at the end of the war became the embryonic Mexican American community.

There is mention of the "westward expansion" in this area of history as well as of "Manifest Destiny;" however, both are presented outside of their relationship to American Indians and Mexicans. There is no recognition that the advocates of Manifest Destiny viewed these groups as racially and culturally inferior and that they suffered a tremendous loss of land, liberty and even life, as a result of this expansion.

Both references above relate to the Latino experience at the third level of representation (Event), since the Hispanic presence is directly implied by the events identified, without there being any specific mention of the group itself.

In the areas of culture, KSA #8.24, there are four references to "racial and ethnic groups" from the seventeenth through the nineteenth centuries. Summarizing these, the student understands the relationships among these groups, analyzes the contributions they made to our national identity, identifies their reasons for immigration and ways in which their conflicts were resolved (Ibid, p. B-25).

All these are worthy objectives for study; however, aside from the contributions statement, it's relevant to note that they are classified under "culture." The dynamic relationships among racial and ethnic groups, their reasons for immigration and their conflicts are not simply a matter of culture, but of multiple social, economic and political factors. So, these very historical phenomena are decontextualized from the historical discussion that relates to wider events, conflicts, and developments and instead placed in "culture," as if they were tangential and not central to the history of the nation.

Nevertheless, since Latinos are categorized as an ethnic minority, there are four instances of Level 4 representations in this KSA, thus providing opportunity or space for Latinos to be included. But, as for all level 4 mentions (Category), this inclusion represents only a potential since teachers are not specifically directed to cover Latinos, Hispanics, or Mexican Americans, let alone give their experience any significant attention.

Outside of these six indirect and potential references to the Latino experience, there are no other KSAs where the Latino presence is even implied. There certainly are some KSAs where the teacher could include aspects or examples of the Latino experience, for example, Culture #8.27A: "describe developments in art, music, literature, drama, and other cultural activities in the history of the United States" (Ibid, p. B-26).

Still, teachers could conceivably cover key eras and genres, without consciously including any Latino contributions, such as from the Mexican muralists and Latino prize-winning poets and novelists. By comparison, it would be difficult to exclude African Americans as easily, due to their foundational influence on popular, mainstream U.S. music and dance.

Thus, we can conclude from the above review that there is no direct mention at all of Latinos or Hispanics as a people in the entire first part of U.S. History TEKS, although their presence or experience do have a few opportunities to be included as a discretional choice of the classroom teacher.

U.S. History Since 1877

Within the seven KSAs dedicated to history in the high school level course, there are four potential items in which the Latino experience could be included. In KSA #1C: "explain the significance of the following dates:

1898, 1914–18, 1929, 1941–1945, and 1957," the first date, 1898, refers to the Spanish American War (Ibid, p. C-2). This conflict involved both Puerto Ricans and Cubans and brought both groups of Latinos, especially the former, into the direct orbit of influence, and direct control, of the United States. The resultant migrations of both groups and the historical, political, and cultural relations between the U.S. and Puerto Rico, as well as that between our nation and Cuba were an eventual result of the Spanish American War (Gonzalez, 2000).

Of course, all of this is a Level 3 mention (Event), since the Cuban and Puerto Rican experiences are only tangentially implied by the date 1898 and its direct reference to this military conflict.

The second item occurs in #2C and is a Level 4 mention (Category) since Latinos are categorically both a minority as well as immigrants: "analyze social issues such as the treatment of minorities, child labor, growth of cities, and problems of immigrants" (Ibid, p. C-2). Here there is an opportunity to deal with some the specific problems and issues that affect Latinos in the context of U.S. history. But again, this is still optional from the teacher's perspective, since Latinos are not directly specified.

The third and fourth items with potential Latino relevance in the history KSAs are in #7 "The student understands the impact of the American civil rights movement." These occur specifically in section B "identify significant leaders of the civil rights movement, including Martin Luther King, Jr." and D: "identify changes in the United States that have resulted from the civil rights movement such as increased participation of minorities in the political process" (Ibid, p. C-4).

That the civil rights movement should be mentioned is positive and necessary, but also to be expected; its absence would have been obviously glaring. However, section B ends quite abruptly, with a semi-colon after the name of Martin Luther King, Jr. and no other names mentioned, as if others were mistakenly or deliberately left out. For every other similar student expectation in the TEKS, several names are always listed, whereas here, there is not even a list of names. Is it that the writers could not think of any others; or is it that they could not agree upon appropriate examples?

Whatever the reason, the opportunity exists to include Latino civil rights leaders such as César Chávez, Antonia Pantoja, and William C. Velasquez. Section B thus is a Level 3 mention (Event), whereby the event, the civil rights movement, implies the presence and participation of Latinos. However, it should be noted that the term "civil rights movement" usually implies only the African American struggle for civil rights, thus further making it unlikely that teachers will even consider the Latino movement which was not as dramatized on the silver screen and which occurred in separate regions of the U.S. among different national origin groups.

Section D is a Level 4 mention (Category) since it implies Latinos categorically as one of those "minorities" who have increased their participation in the political process as a result of the civil rights movement.

In addition to these four indirect mentions of Latinos in the history KSA in this second part of U.S. History TEKS, there two others in geography, and four in culture where, as in the first part, Latinos are indirectly alluded to categorically as immigrants and as an ethnoracial group. In geography, #9A, students are expected to "analyze the effects of physical and human geographic factors on major events including the building of the Panama Canal" (Ibid, p. C-5). That process clearly involved Panamanians and classifies this item as a Level 3 mention. It is also relevant to a very recent and significant event: the U.S. transfer of the Panama Canal's control to Panama on December 31, 1999.

In the next KSA, #10B, students are expected to "analyze the effects of changing demographic patterns resulting from immigration to the United States" (Ibid). This is an obvious possibility for including Latinos, albeit at a Level 3, considering that they already are, as documented by the 2000 Census, the largest ethnoracial minority in the United States, due in large measure to immigration.

Under the umbrella of minority groups adapting to life in the U.S. and contributing "to our national identity," Culture KSA #21 has a general description as well as three relevant sections, A, B and C where Latinos could be directly included. These require students to explain actions taken by these groups to expand economic opportunities and political rights and to explain Americanization efforts, as well as to analyze these groups' contributions that have helped shape the national identity. All three expectations can generate much knowledge about the Latino experience, but since Latinos are implied rather than specified, these are Level 4 (Category) mentions in which Latinos are included only at the discretion and choice of the classroom teacher.

From the above review of the second part of USHTEKS, it is clear, as was the case in the first part, that again there is no direct mention of Latinos or any national-origin Latino sub-group in the entire scope of TEKS for both courses of U.S. history. Neither is there mention of a single Latino individual. The second part, however, did contain in its contents as many as ten indirect potential references to Latinos categorically as a racial, ethnic or immigrant group, or by virtue of an event or movement identified.

With six in the first and ten in the second, there are at least sixteen opportunities for U.S. history teachers to integrate even under the TEKS as written, some aspects of the Latino experience in the curriculum.

Unfortunately, these remain as opportunities only, since teachers are not directed to include Latinos by name in the written guidelines.

The undeniable and astounding fact remains that no specific mention is made at all of Hispanics, Latinos, Mexican Americans or any Latino group in the entire TEKS for U.S. history. Neither is there a single Latino/Hispanic individual identified by name therein. Is this merely a coincidence, a case of neglectful oversight, or deliberate policy?

Those questions are beyond the scope of this study. Nevertheless, in the next section, we will review these TEKS to determine where and how African Americans and American Indians are mentioned, and make comparisons with the representation of Latinos.

Please refer to the Appendix A for tables on Latino, African American and American Indian representation in both parts of USHTEKS.

African Americans and American Indians

In the first part of USHTEKS, through Reconstruction, given the historical importance of slavery and the Civil War, as expected, African Americans receive the most attention of all three groups with twelve relevant items. American Indians have five items, most of which are indirect references.

On African Americans, there is a Level 1 reference to Frederick Douglass in Citizenship KSA #8.23B, among other "significant political, social, and military leaders." No American Indian or Latino leader is mentioned by name. African Americans are named as a group, a Level 2 mention, and referred to as both "slaves and free blacks" in History #8.7B, which draws specific attention to them directing students to "compare the effects of political, economic, and social factors on slaves and free blacks." This is within the context of KSA #8.7, which makes reference to factors leading up the Civil War.

In addition, there are at least seven Level 3 references to African Americans in the following KSAs and topics: History #8.7C: "impact of slavery"; History #8.8B: the Emancipation Proclamation; History #8.9C: the impact of Reconstruction on different groups in the South; Economics #8.13B: "growth of the slave trade, and the spread of slavery;" Government #8.17B: the impact of the 13th, 14th and 15th amendments; Government #8.19B: impact of the Dred Scott v Sanford case; and Culture #8.25A: "the historical development of the abolitionist movement." The three Level 4 references made concerning African Americans are all in the area of Culture #8.24, and sections C and D which deal with the relationships between racial and ethnic groups, how their conflicts were resolved and the contributions they made to our national identity.

Three of the five references to American Indians are contained in KSA #8.24. All are Level 4 (Categorical), as were the four for Latinos in this area. The only specific Level 2 mention of an American Indian group was in History #8.5G, wherein "Cherokee Indians" are named in the context of their resettlement during the Jacksonian era. That same section also contains a Level 3 reference to "federal and state Indian policies." Thus, the overall numbers of indirect references to American Indians and Latinos are comparable, although no specific Latino group is named.

It is also interesting to note that the term "Indian" is used instead of either "Native American" or "American Indian," and that "blacks" (with a small "b") is used to refer to African Americans, yet nowhere in the TEKS is there any mention of "whites" as a category. Nevertheless, we can assume that European immigrants are included as racial-ethnic minorities or immigrants.

As in the first part of USHTEKS, in the second part African Americans not only receive more attention, meager as it is, than either Latinos or American Indians, but also have three (Level 1) specific individuals mentioned: W.E. B. DuBois in History #4B; Martin Luther King, Jr. in History #7B; and Shirley Chisholm in Citizenship #19B. The African American presence or experience is also directly implied in #7 with the civil rights movement and the Civil Rights Act of 1964; whereas in section #7D, African Americans are implied categorically, as are Latinos, as one of the "minorities" which increased participation in the political process. There is also mention in Culture #20 B of the "Harlem Renaissance," in direct reference to a pivotal African American cultural and intellectual development.

In conclusion, American Indians are the least represented of the three groups. African Americans, with the most representation, are mentioned by name as a group, and as they should be, are accorded a place in the historical narrative. More importantly, African Americans have four significant individuals identified as worthy of knowing about in Texas classrooms, whereas Latinos and American Indians have none.

By contrast, given their relative numbers and influence, Latinos are the most underrepresented of these three groups in these TEKS for U.S. history. There is no reference ever made to them as Latinos, Hispanics, Mexican Americans or any specific national-origin group. Neither is any individual Latino mentioned by name, although opportunities for their inclusion under other categories such as "immigrant" or "minority" do exist within the content and structure of TEKS.

Chapter Four

Textbooks: Still in the Margins

METHODS USED TO ANALYZE TEXTBOOKS

Three of the six U.S. history textbooks adopted by TEA and in current use for high school were reviewed for their Latino representation in this content analysis study. The ScottForesman text was selected in particular because it was the officially adopted textbook by Northside I.S.D., thus the text being used by the sixteen teachers I interviewed. The other two texts were selected because they were also published by major, well-established national textbook companies and would appropriately serve as comparables. The reviewed textbooks are:

> Berkin, Carol, et al. (1992). *American voices: A history of the United States, Volume II: 1865 to the present.* Glenview, IL: ScottForesman.
>
> Davidson, J.W., Lytle, M.H. and Stoff, M.B. (1992). *American journey: The quest for liberty since 1865.* Englewood Cliffs, NJ: Prentice Hall.
>
> Garraty, John. (1992). *The story of America, Vol. 2: 1865 to the present.* Austin, TX: Holt, Rinehart and Winston.

Since both quantitative and qualitative data was gathered from each text, Garcia's (1980) model is well suited for the task. Following Garcia's approach, the collection of quantitative data consisted of counting the number of sentences in the textbook with content relating to each of the three largest national origin Latino groups in the U.S., namely, Mexican-American, Puerto Rican, or Cuban-American. A fourth category of Hispanic (or Latino) would be used for sentences relating to Hispanic Americans as a general group and/or of other Latin American nationalities.

These sentences were also categorized by the type of content they cover. In Garcia's system there are seven general topics, thus each sentence was categorized according to the extent to which it

1. described why each group immigrated to the U.S.
2. described when each group immigrated and where initial contacts began
3. gave a historical perspective to the problems and accomplishments associated with each group.
4. described key events and issues which are crucial in gaining an understanding of the group.
5. provided content that notes each group's shared and unique characteristics and experiences.
6. included descriptions of leaders and their contributions to the American scene.
7. included content describing other experiences of the group.

(Garcia, 1980, p. 109).

By identifying topical categories for these Latino-related sentences, Garcia established a quantitative foundation which could help guide the qualitative assessment of the content describing each Latino group.

It's important to note that in this textbook content analysis, sentences that serve as captions to paintings, illustrations, tables, etc. were included in the total number of sentences counted as were direct quotations from leaders or from literary sources not part of the main narrative. Also, note that some texts may contain more than sentences, but several pages and entire sections directly discussing Latin America or Central America as a region, or individual Latino nations. These are not included in the sentence count above, although it would be a worthy task for future research. This effort is focused on the presence of Latinos living in the United States.

The quantitative data will be displayed on a table indicating the number of sentences categorized by topic and by national origin group. Thus, each textbook will have a unique quantitative profile based on the number of sentences it contains related to Latinos, categorized by specific group and topic. The topics and groups receiving the most and the least attention could then be determined and compared among the various textbooks.

The very identification of Hispanic-related material is a task in itself and requires several steps to ensure it is adequately done. Garcia suggested a procedure for doing this that can be summarized as follows:

1. Turn to the index of each text, note pages listed under each target group, review these pages, and identify the content.
2. By skimming the text, identify and review non-indexed pages that describe each group, and classify them.
3. Review all identified data and match it with appropriate question.
4. Classify under the general group "Hispanic" all sentences that describe more than one of the three groups (Ibid, p. 110).

I added an additional step between Garcia's step 1 and 2, which would be to look in the index for events, organizations, concepts or any other item which related to the experience of Latinos as a whole or any of the three national origin groups. These, of course, would then be reviewed, categorized, and included with all the other sentences.

METHODS FOR TEXTBOOK DATA ANALYSIS

The amount of content, specifically the number of sentences, for each of the seven topical categories of information, was noted. The analysis was focused on those topics which received the most or the least attention. Also analyzed was how the quantity of content was distributed among the four target groups, as well as whether there were differential distributions of content among the seven questions for each group. This permitted me to determine, for example, if coverage of the three groups differed widely in the amount of content used to describe when, how and why each group immigrated to the United States.

The qualitative analysis, though not exactly replicating Garcia's, is consistent with his approach. For this study I noted the extent to which individual sentences or entire paragraphs, pages or sections, met the following five criteria:

1. Factual accuracy
2. Inclusion of key leaders, dates, events, issues, or contributions
3. Presentation of Hispanic views or perspectives
4. Agency attributed to Hispanic leaders, organizations, or people
5. Connections made between the past and present

Although the very nature of the information expressed in these sentences may make some criteria more or less relevant, at least one of the five criteria provided an appropriate basis for an assessment of quality. Also, every sentence or group of sentences in a paragraph or page could actually reflect two or more of these criteria, making these more meaningful for the authentic and complete telling of Latino history in the U.S. Conversely, some sentences might meet none of these criteria.

It is important to emphasize that both quantity and quality have value in assessing how well these U.S. history textbooks cover the presence, experience and contributions of Latinos. While no formula was devised for balancing or integrating quantitative and qualitative aspects of each textbook, both will be noted, described and discussed, and a final assessment will consider both the number of sentences as well as their level of quality.

PRESENTATION OF DATA

This report includes information on each of the textbooks reviewed and an overall assessment as to how accurately and objectively each textbook covered Latino content. The discussion on qualitative content and analysis is presented using the five thematic criteria, and noting how well these were fulfilled by each of the sentences or groups of sentences.

The quantitative content is presented in table form, similar to the format used by Garcia. The following sample excerpt from a larger table shows how this data is presented for one textbook and three topics. The figures represent the number of sentences for each topic and group, with H=Hispanic or Latino, MA=Mexican American, PR=Puerto Rican, and CA=Cuban American. Notice that subtotals by topic and by group could thus be calculated and compared across the three textbooks.

Table of Sentences for Textbook A

	H	MA	PR	CA	Subtotals
Topic #1	7	11	5	4	27
Topic #2	5	3	2	0	10
Topic #3	7	9	4	3	23
ETC. . . .					
Subtotals	19+	23+	11+	7+	60+

DATA FROM UNITED STATES HISTORY TEXTBOOKS

Frequency tables were produced for each of the three books, using the seven topics described above and three national origin groups as well as Latino or Hispanic in general. Reproduced below are these three tables which also include totals for each category, and for the overall number of sentences in each textbook. Please refer to Appendix B: Textbook Tables to view the following three tables.

Textbook Table 1
Sentences by Topic & Hispanic National Origin in Garraty/Holt R&W

Topics	H/L	MA	PR	CA	Totals
1: Why Imm	0	5	1	1	7
2: When/Where	3	9	1	2	15
3: Prblms/Accmp	35	32	6	5	78
4: Events/Issues	21	12	5	4	42
5: Chrcts/Exprns	15	43	31	2	91
6: Leaders	0	27	5	0	32
7: Other Exprns	0	0	0	0	0
Totals by Origin	74	128	49	14	265

Textbook Table 2
Sentences by Topic & Hispanic National Origin in Davidson/Prentice Hall

Topics	H/L	MA	PR	CA	Totals
1: Why Imm	1	7	0	1	9
2: When/Where	0	24	6	2	32
3: Prblms/Accmp	20	20	0	10	50
4: Events/Issues	7	17	4	0	28
5: Chrcts/Exprns	26	90	6	2	124
6: Leaders	0	132	1	0	133
7: Other Exprns	0	0	0	0	0
Totals by Origin	54	290	17	15	376

Textbook Table 3
Sentences by Topic & Hispanic National Origin in Berkin et al./Scott Foresman

Topics	H/L	MA	PR	CA	Totals
1: Why Imm	0	7	0	0	7
2: When/Where	6	5	2	0	13
3: Prblms/Accmp	11	20	0	0	31
4: Events/Issues	10	7	8	0	25
5: Chrcts/Exprns	14	58	6	1	79
6: Leaders	0	21	4	0	25
7: Other Exprns	0	0	0	0	0
Totals by Origin	41	118	20	1	180

DISCUSSION OF TEXTBOOK TABLES

Table 1: Garraty/Holt

As reflected in their population numbers, Mexican Americans, or Mexican origin Hispanics, have the largest number of sentences directly related to their history in the U.S., 128, followed by Puerto Ricans, 49, and then Cuban Americans, 14. Seventy-four sentences also focus on Hispanic Americans as a group.

For both Mexican Americans (43) and Puerto Ricans (31), and in the sub-totals (91), the topic category that received most attention was #5 dealing with unique characteristics and experiences of the group. This was followed by topic 3, providing historical perspectives on the group's problems and accomplishments. For Cuban Americans, however, topic 3 had the most sentences, followed by topic 4, significant events and issues. This same pattern, with topic 3 receiving the most attention followed by topic 4, is reflected in sentences dealing with Hispanics as a group.

Several sections in this text especially one on the "Revolution in Mexico" (pp. 280–81), relate to Latin America. Two other sections worthy of note in this text comprise the final chapter: "Latin America and the Caribbean" (pp. 595–609), and "Latin America: 1960s—1990s" (pp. 610–621). All these sections do provide some basic information that increases student's understanding of this region's relationship with the United States and the issues this has generated.

Table 2: Davidson/Prentice Hall

As expected, more sentences relate to the Mexican American experience (290); but to such an overwhelming extent, however, that this goes beyond Mexican Americans' proportion of the Latino population overall. At the same time, Puerto Ricans receive very little attention in this text (17), similar to Cubans (15), despite Puerto Ricans' considerably larger numbers.

In terms of the topics covered for Mexican Americans, leaders (topic 6) have more sentences (132) than any other category of information, followed by topic 5, unique characteristics and experiences (90). Subtotals for the two topics with the most sentences follow that same pattern. It is significant to note that this predominant and laudable attention given to Mexican American leaders does not carry over to Puerto Rican (1) and Cuban (0) leaders, who are practically left out of the narrative altogether.

Of the fifty-four sentences related to Latinos as a whole, almost half (26) are about topic 5, followed by topic 3, problems and accomplishments. Ten of the fifteen sentences related to Cuban Americans are on topic 3, whereas for Puerto Ricans, a different pattern exists: the seventeen sentences cover three topics in more balanced proportions with topic 5 and topic 2, (when and where migration occurred), having six sentences each and topic 4, (significant events and issues) having four sentences.

Thus, for each of the three national origin groups, a distinct pattern emerges in terms of the distribution of sentences over topical areas, and none of these three patterns is similar to that of sentences which relate to Latinos as a whole. The most obvious and revealing aspect of this sentence distribution is the overwhelming number of sentences dedicated to Mexican Americans in comparison to that of Puerto Ricans, Cubans and to Hispanics as a group.

Table 3: Berkin/Scott Foresman

As reflected in both other textbooks, and consistent with their larger proportion of the Latino population, Mexican Americans (118) received more attention than the other two groups. Here, as in the other two texts, considerably fewer (20) sentences are dedicated to Puerto Ricans, but unlike the other two, only one sentence is focused directly on Cuban Americans.

In terms of topics, for Mexican Americans (58), Hispanics in general (14), in the sub-totals (79), topic 5, unique characteristics and experiences, had considerably more sentences than any other topic. Overall, topics 3, 4, and 6 also had twenty-five or more sentences each.

In addition to the sentences in the main body of the textbook, there were special, optional reading sections which covered aspects of the Latino experience. Under the category of "American Literature" or "Source Readings," were several passages written by Hispanic authors. Among those was a piece on page 488 by Puerto Rican writer, Piri Thomas; another literary selection on page 638 was by Cuban American, Pulitzer Prize winner Oscar Hijuelos; on page 642, a passage by the late Mexican American educator, Tomás Rivera; and on pages 882–83, there is a poem by Mexican American poet, Teresa Polomo Acosta.

Cuban revolutionary leader, José Martí, is featured with a short biography and poem on page 312, and the Mexican novelist, Mariano Azuela, has an excerpt of his novel printed on pages 314–315. There is also an interesting section on Diego Rivera, the Mexican muralist on pages 484–85; and on page 828, is a section, "Highlights of American Life," on the South American educator, Jaime Escalante and his work as documented in the film, *Stand and Deliver.*

Perhaps the most significant of these optional readings, in terms of U.S. Latinos, is a statement by César Chavez accompanied by a large color photo of him with a caption and discussion questions, on pages 720–21.

All of these optional readings do much to enhance the students' understanding of the Hispanic experience, but the extent to which teachers use these resources beyond the text itself is not certain, and therefore not part of the sentence count included in the above table. In a qualitative sense, as well as quantitative, these sections and their associated suggested activities do make a difference in the overall presentation of Latinos in the textbook and should be considered when making comparisons with other textbooks.

Finally, in terms of quantity, it should be noted that this text also has a "Biographical Dictionary," beginning on page 936, which includes the biographies of four Hispanic Americans: César Chavez, William Velasquez, Lauro Cavazos, and Antonia Coello Novello, the latter two being the first Hispanic cabinet appointees to lead their departments.

Contrast and Comparison of Tables

In terms of the total number of sentences dedicated to the Latino experience in the narrative, captions and quotes there is considerable variation among the three texts. The Davidson text has over twice as many of these sentences (376) as does the Berkin text (180), although if the optional readings related to Latinos in the latter text were counted in Berkin, the difference would not be as dramatic.

In the Garraty text, most of the 265 Latino related sentences are, as in the other two textbooks, focused on Mexican Americans; this is to be expected, reflecting both demographic and historical realities. Yet these Mexi can American related sentences in Garraty (128) represent about 48% of the total dedicated to Latinos. In the Berkin textbook, the Mexican American related sentences (118) represent about 66% of the total sentences in that text, and in the Davidson textbook, the Mexican American sentences, (290) represent about 77% percent of the total sentences related to Latinos.

In the representation of Puerto Ricans and Cubans, the second and third largest groups, the three textbooks also differ in their relative coverage. In the Garraty text, almost 19% of the sentences are related to Puerto Ricans, and about 5% are about Cuban Americans. The Berkin text dedicates about 11% of its sentences to Puerto Ricans, and a mere .6% or just over one-half percent to Cuban Americans, in essence, only one sentence. In the Davidson text only about 5% of the sentences related to Puerto Ricans and about 4% to Cuban Americans. Thus the Garraty textbook does a better job of presenting a more balanced distribution of attention to these three groups commensurate with their relative populations than do the other two textbooks.

In terms of the distribution of sentences by topical areas, both the Berkin and the Garraty textbooks had more sentences regarding topic 5, the shared, unique characteristics of Latino groups, followed by topic 3, a historical perspective on the groups' problems and accomplishments. In contrast to this, the Davidson text has more sentences describing leaders and their contribution to the American scene, topic 6, then followed by topics 5 and 3 in terms of sentence count.

In this regard, it is important to note that of the one hundred thirty-three sentences in Davidson regarding Hispanic leaders, all but one were about Mexican American leaders, again illustrating the unbalanced treatment of Puerto Ricans and Cuban Americans in this text.

VISUALS IN THE THREE TEXTBOOKS

In addition to the sentences from the narrative and other sources, there are also some significant visuals related to Latinos in the three textbooks. All the Latino-related visuals of each text are number-listed and briefly described below with page numbers indicated as well. A final section will compare these across textbooks.

Visuals in Garraty/Holt, R&W

1. America's Hispanic Heritage: A "Portfolio" of ten items, mostly paintings, depicting aspects of the Hispanic cultural and historic

heritage, accompanied by informative captions and a five sentence text, 26–29

2. Painting by Gentilz depicting a Southwestern Spanish-style settlement with caption to accompany text on the settling of the Southwest, 89

3. Color painting by Walker: "California Vaqueros" in full dress, 106

4. Two maps: One of the Greater Antilles: Cuba, Haiti/Dominican Republic, Jamaica, and Puerto Rico; and another of Puerto Rico by itself, showing three major cities on the island, 216

5. Color photo: Group of Cuban immigrants waving U.S. flags, 552

6. Two photos: One b&w photo of Mexican braceros in the field, and another color photo of César Chavez, smiling, including the NFWA symbol in the background with a "Huelga" sign, 55

7. Two photos: Both b&w of two children at New York's Puerto Rican Day Parade; one photo shows a boy with baseball suit, cap and bat, the other a girl holding a Puerto Rican flag, 560

8. One bar graph: Selected Characteristics of Hispanic Americans and Non-Hispanic Americans. Five groups, Mexican Americans, Cubans, Puerto Ricans, Central/South Americans, and Non-Hispanic Americans, are compared along four measures: Average Years of Schooling; Average Family Income, Percent Unemployed, Percent of Families Below Poverty Level. The chart is quite colorful, accompanied by a caption and a citation of source and date for the information: Current Population Reports, 1987, 561

Overall, the paintings and the photographs depicting Latino people, leaders, and historic periods are quite authentic. The "portfolio" of mostly Hispanic American paintings was well done and the bar graph illustrated a considerable amount of accurate information.

Visuals in Davidson/Prentice Hall

1. A color painting, without title or name of artist, of a scene of vaqueros with horses in a corral, 103

2. Map: the Spanish American War in the Caribbean, 269

3. Map: the U.S. in the Caribbean: 1898–1917, 286

4. B&W Photograph: of Mexican Americans on strike, the pecan Shellers in San Antonio, led by Emma Tenayuca, shown in the photo and mentioned in the caption, 423

5. Photograph: Dr. Hector P. Garcia, founder of the American G.I. Forum, with President L. B. Johnson, 571
6. Photograph, color: Of a Mexican American mural on the wall of a building in an apartment project, 572
7. Map of the U.S.A.: of the Hispanic Population in the U.S., with all 50 states color-coded by percentage of Hispanic population, 678
8. Photograph: of Gloria Estefan, Cuban American pop and salsa star

Most of the visuals related to Hispanics in this textbook are either photographs or maps. The latter are quite accurate; especially useful is the population map on page 678, showing Latino population by state.

However, there is a problem in that over 3.5 million U.S. citizens in Puerto Rico are excluded from the count since the island of Puerto Rico is not shown, as it should be, albeit as a "territory" of the U.S.

The photographs are not remarkable except for the black and white of Mexican American pecan shellers on strike, including their leader, Emma Tenayuca, a distinguished union organizer in San Antonio in the late 1930s.

Visuals in Berkin/Scott Foresman

1. An illustration: of Louisiana's Spanish Governor Bernardo de Gálvez, who helped fight the British during the American Revolution, 24
2. Map: of the military events of the American Revolution includes caption on Gálvez, 53
3. Color Photo: of César Chavez, larger size, 72
4. Color Map: Caribbean during the Spanish American War, 294
5. Color Cartoon: of Puerto Rico as a little girl attempting to enter the U.S. house while being threatened by a big brown wolf, 297
6. B&W drawing: of Cuban American rebels at a meeting in NYC, 313
7. B&W photo: poor Mexican American working woman, 336.
8. Sepia photo: Mexican Americans herding sheep (Depression), 444.
9. B&W photo: Mexican American teens learning food catering, 481
10. Color photo: César Chavez with other union members, 715
11. Color map and graph: the map of the U.S. with Alaska and Hawaii shows the relative population of Hispanics in each state

The graph illustrates the number of immigrants arriving in the U.S. from 1950 through 1985 from four sources: Mexico, Cuba, Puerto Rico, and Other Hispanic Countries, 864

12. Three color photos: of Lauro Cavazos, Dr. Antonio Novello, and of two Texas high school students bringing school supplies to Mexican children, 865

Photographs comprise the bulk of visuals related to Hispanics in Berkin. Several leaders are highlighted in these photos and the few maps do contain useful and accurate information. The color cartoon on Puerto Rico as a little girl, threatened by a ravenous wolf (Spain) (297) although small, was especially impactful because the caption explains that, contrary to the cartoon's implications, before the Spanish American War, the islanders had been set to gain a parliamentary government under Spain.

Generally, the visuals are realistic and representative portrayals of Latinos.

Comparisons of Visuals Among Textbooks

Looking at the quality of the Latino-related visuals in all three texts, it is reasonable to conclude that Davidson has the weakest presentation and that Garraty offers a larger, more diverse and more authentic collection of photographs, paintings, and illustrations.

All three texts have demographic maps and charts as well. Garraty has an informative bar graph comparing selective characteristics among Hispanics and non-Hispanics. Davidson has a small demographic map of the Latino population by state in the U.S. A similar map also appears in Berkin, but it is accompanied by a three dimensional graph showing numbers of immigrants from various nations or regions of Latin America from 1950 to 1985. The Berkin graph is colorful and very useful in terms of historical context and meaning. Overall both Berkin and Garraty have better quality visuals related to Latinos than does Davidson.

QUALITATIVE ASPECTS OF EACH TEXTBOOK

To analyze the qualitative aspects of the written text, which is the narrative itself as well as integrated quotes, the five criteria mentioned in the Methods section above were applied.

1. Factual accuracy
2. Inclusion of key leaders, dates, events, issues, and contributions
3. Presentation of Latino views or perspectives

4. Agency attributed to Latino leaders, organizations, or people
5. Connections made between past & present

Garraty/Holt, R&W

Looking first at the longer sections written about Hispanics in the textbook, on pages 557—559, *Mexican Americans Increase Their Numbers,* the facts presented regarding demographics, leaders, groups and events, are accurate. Key leaders, namely César Chávez, and the nature of his struggle are included in the narrative, and the perspective of Rodolfo "Gorky" Gonzalez is presented in an excerpt from his epic poem "Yo Soy Joaquín"/"I am Joaquín." Thus, the first three criteria were met.

As far as attributing agency is concerned, again the narrative inclusion of union activism and organizing done by Chávez and by union members fulfills the fourth criteria. Finally, the connections between past and present are not stated in the text, however, the issues of farmworker rights, and of Chicano identity are still relevant today; thus it is left to the teacher to make these obvious connections.

Immediately following is another section, *Other Hispanic Newcomers,* which provides background information on Puerto Ricans, Cubans, Central and South Americans in the U.S. Most of the data provided on Puerto Ricans is accurate. However, the authors drew parallels between Puerto Ricans and European immigrants without mentioning the factors which distinguished them, other than the citizenship status of Puerto Ricans. These factors include the colonial status of the island as a U.S. territory seized in the Spanish American War and the role American corporations played in the island's economy, compelling many Puerto Ricans to emigrate.

Nevertheless, most of the background on Cuban Americans especially regarding their reasons for immigrating were quite accurate. Overall, the information in the text and on the chart is factually correct.

Key Latino leaders, namely Herman Badillo, and Fidel Castro are presented, and some significant issues and events are included in the narrative. There is no discussion, however, of the perspectives of these leaders, outside of Fidel Castro's self-labeling as a communist and some Cubans' opposition to him. Yet, agency is attributed to Castro and other Cubans, as well as to Badillo and to "many Puerto Ricans (who) were able to improve their lives" (p. 560).

Some connections are made to the present through the inclusion of demographic information from 1987, and in statements such as, "Hispanic political influence has continued to grow" (p. 561) Thus, in this section on "Other Hispanics," all but the third criteria are fulfilled.

On pages 177–78, there is a literary passage from *Among My People,* a book by Mexican American author, Jovita Gonzalez which describes life in a south Texas Hispanic community. Due to the autobiographical nature of these sentences, one can assume general, but not specific, factual accuracy. That is, the setting and traditions described are accurate, but the specific sequence of events may not, and need not be.

As expected, no key leaders events or contributions are presented, no special agency is attributed, and no connections are deliberately made to the present. However, an Hispanic lifestyle and perspective are described, and their values are implied. Thus this section fulfills the first and third criteria.

The last significant passage in this text is on pages 295—296, and it focuses on Mexican Americans and Mexican immigrants during the first quarter of the 20th century. Included as part of a section on *Labor in Wartime* (World War I), these sentences do provide some useful and factual information on the reasons and conditions confronting workers of Mexican descent. They also include key events and leaders, such as Ezekial Cabeza de Baca, who in 1916 was elected governor of New Mexico, the first Hispanic American governor in the U.S., and also Octaviano Larrazolo, who became the first Hispanic American elected to the Senate in 1928.

No clear Hispanic perspective is presented in this short passage, and no obvious connections are made to the present, but agency is certainly attributed to Mexican American workers and leaders. Thus, these sentences do fulfill the first, second and fourth criteria.

From the above, it is reasonable to consider that the major passages and sections about Latinos in the Garraty textbook do present overall an authentic and accurate portrait of the Latino experience in the U.S.

Davidson/Prentice Hall

There are several passages or sections which focus on the Latino experience in this textbook. On pages 102–3, the rise of cattle ranching and cowboys is covered. The Spanish, Mexicans and Mexican Americans are credited for their establishment of and involvement in the ranching lifestyle of the West. More details on the Mexican *vaquero* and his contributions are covered in a special *Life in America* section titled: "Spanish Heritage of the Cowboy," which included three discussion questions as well as a color illustration. Thus, this section fulfills three of the five qualitative criteria. It is factually accurate (criteria #1), includes key contributions (#2), and attributes agency (#4).

Under a section entitled *Others Bypassed by Prosperity,* the text discusses, on pages 344–46, the economic conditions of Mexican immigrants during the early 1900s. Together with the following section, *Juan—A Solo in Chicago,* the authors provide information as to why Mexicans immigrated and the challenges many of them confronted, especially as single men. The information is accurate, a key event (the Mexican Revolution) is included, an Hispanic perspective is presented, and agency is attributed to Mexican immigrant workers who overcome many obstacles to establish viable communities. The first four criteria are met in this section.

On pages 421–22, the section *Mexican Americans in the 1930s,* dedicates three paragraphs to describe immigration to the Southwest, deportation of Mexican American families, and the involvement of the Mexican American in both agricultural and industrial unions. The facts presented are valid, key events and issues are included, a Latina labor organizer's perspective is quoted, and agency is attributed to Mexican origin workers. Again, as in the previous section reviewed, the first four criteria are met.

The section *Hispanics,* on pages 570–71, followed by one on *Forms of Discrimination,* pages 572—73, represents the most comprehensive treatment of Hispanics in this textbook. There are sub-sections on Cubans and Puerto Ricans, as well as Mexican Americans in the *Hispanics* section, and on "The fight for equality" and "Gains" in the section on discrimination.

Overall, the information is factual, and two key Mexican American leaders, Chávez, and José Angel Gutierrez, founder of the Raza Unida Party, are included. In a special "An American Portrait" section, Dr. Hector Perez Garcia, Mexican American founder of the American GI Forum, is featured in a brief biography and also pictured with President L.B. Johnson.

The perspectives of Latinos are certainly presented, especially in response to discrimination, and agency is attributed to them as they struggled, generally successfully, to gain their rights. Finally, a connection is made with the present in the final few sentences of the "Gains" section which asks questions still relevant today, such as, "How much should they (Hispanics) adopt the customs of mainstream America?" and "How much should they work to preserve their own ethnic ways?" (573) Thus, all five qualitative criteria are well fulfilled in these two sections.

On pages 777–79 in a section, "When You're Small," César Chávez provides a narrative of the working and living conditions his family confronted as migrant workers during the Depression. Factual accuracy is not at issue, and all the other qualitative criteria, except for making a direct connection with present conditions, are met well by this selection.

In another section on *Hispanics* on pages 677–79, the authors attempt to bring the discussion of this group up to date, focusing on cultural influences, population and other demographics. The following section, *"Melting Pot" or "Salad Bowl,"* the two distinct perspectives on assimilation are discussed briefly ending with a quite a few sentences on the issue of bilingual education. Again, factual accuracy is not a problem and some connections are made with the present and future regarding the Hispanic presence. However, there is not enough written here to attribute agency, present an Hispanic perspective, or include any key leaders, events, or issues, except for that of bilingual education.

Moreover in this regard, bilingual education is described in one sentence, followed by four sentences presenting opposition to it. Nevertheless, not one statement is made to present the arguments in favor of bilingual education. Here is an example of where an Hispanic perspective is sorely needed for balance and accuracy. This bias against presenting balanced information on bilingual education, though quite common in the mass media, is inexcusable in a textbook.

Compared to those which appear earlier in this text, these later sections have certain weaknesses, and that's unfortunate. If anything, Hispanic influence is likely to grow even stronger in the present and future than what it was in the past, making appropriate representation of this group even more essential. Nevertheless, despite these weaknesses in these later sections, overall, most of the sections dealing with Hispanics in this textbook provide valid and authentic information to the reader.

Berkin/Scott Foresman

There is considerably less textual narrative in this than in the other two textbooks, although there were a number of optional readings, discussed above, which overall were of good quality. Among the more significant sections in the narrative itself is one on the growth of cattle ranching and the birth of the cowboy on pages 173–74. Therein a few statements are made about how Americans borrowed methods from the *vaquero,* as well as the Spanish words associated with cattle ranching. These statements are factual and do recognize a key contributions Mexicans make to the economic development of the West.

In the context of a discussion on American imperialism, there is coverage on pages 297–98 of how Cuba and Puerto Rico "came under the American flag." Most descriptions of the events, some in significant detail, are accurate, and there are also some important explanations provided on the evolving citizenship status of Puerto Ricans from 1900 through 1917. Key dates, events and issues are included, although there is no mention of the views of Cuban and Puerto Rican leaders, revolutionaries who had been advocating for independence from Spain for decades and were suspicious of U.S. imperialist tendencies.

However, little or no agency is attributed to Hispanic people or leaders throughout the author's discussion of imperialism. Finally, there is no discussion of how these events after the Spanish American War are connected with the presence of Puerto Ricans and Cubans in the contemporary body politic and society of this nation today. Thus, only the first two qualitative criteria are met by this section.

In a section entitled *Mexicans migrated to the Southwest* on pages 336–37, the authors provide three reasons why immigrants from Mexico came to the Southwest from 1910 to 1921. More than half of this section, however, is dedicated to relating the experiences of Mexican American leader, Ernesto Galarza, as a new immigrant in Sacramento, California. Most of the information is valid. A key leader, dates and events are included; Galarza's views are expressed; and agency is attributed to Latinos. Four of the five criteria are met herein. There was one error, the Mexican Revolution was, or began, in 1910, not 1911, as stated on page 336.

Another section on pages 444–45 explained how *Many Mexican Americans were forced to leave the country,* during the early 1930s and Depression years. The job discrimination and forced deportations endured by Mexican Americans during this period are described. The facts are accurate, and some key issues are considered, but no connections with the present are made; no agency is attributed in response to these conditions; and no Hispanic perspectives on these issues are expressed. Thus, only two criteria are met in this section.

In a short, three-paragraph section, "The New Deal and Mexican Americans" on page 480, the authors describe how the New Deal programs impacted Mexican Americans and how other conditions prevented them from fully benefiting from these opportunities. The facts herein are accurately presented and key events are included, but the section is too short to elaborate on any of the other three criteria.

A more comprehensive treatment of *Hispanic Americans* is provided on pages 714–15, focusing on their various responses to the "turbulent climate of the late 1960s . . ." (p. 714). Following some basic demographic data in terms of the concentration of the three largest groups, the authors discuss some of the civil rights issues confronted by Hispanic leaders during these years. The facts are accurate; again César Chávez is highlighted as are some key issues and events; Hispanic views on bilingualism and assimilation are expressed; and agency is attributed to Hispanic leaders and activists. The first four criteria are met well in this section.

The last major section in our review, on pages 863–65, provides perhaps the most comprehensive and updated treatment of Latinos in this textbook. Titled, *"The Hispanic American population grew enormously in the 1980s,"* the authors begin the discussion with demographic data, especially focusing on legal and illegal migration and population growth. Then in a sub-section on "Increased political power," the narrative focuses on two high level Hispanic appointees, Lauro F. Cavazos, a Mexican American, as Secretary of Education, and Dr. Antonia Coello Novello, a Puerto Rican, as Surgeon General. Both were the first Hispanics, and in Novello's case, also the first woman, to head their cabinet posts.

Finally, the last sub-section, "Increased voter registration," focuses on the successes Hispanics have had in national, state and local politics through increased voting and political participation. Willie Velasquez, Mexican American founder of Southwest Voter Registration Project, is also included in the discussion. Overall, this final section, enhanced by photographs, maps and graphs, does provide considerable information. Key leaders are included as are certain issues; the views of these leaders are expressed; and agency is attributed. The first four qualitative criteria are well met in these final section and the issues and topics covered, such as illegal immigration, the drop-out rate, and AIDS are still relevant today.

Qualitative Comparisons Among Textbooks

It is quite difficult to make very specific comparisons among the three texts in terms of quality, yet the extent to which the passages in each text meet the five criteria could help in this task. In a comparison of the quality of longer passages related to Latinos in this texts, for example, it becomes evident that in the Davidson textbook most of these meet four or more of the five qualitative criteria.

Averaging out the ratings (on a scale from 1 to 5) for all six major Latino-related sections in the Davidson/Prentice Hall text would yield a 3.67 rating. Doing the same with the sections in the Garraty/Holt text generates a rating of 3.25, and for the Berkin/Scott Foresman text, that rating would be a 2.7.

Yet, these numbers only reveal part of the qualitative aspect. The Berkin textbook, for example, has the courage to deal honestly with certain issues such as discrimination, forced deportations, and political empowerment as well as or better than the other two texts. There is even a discussion in Berkin of "American imperialism" in the context of the Spanish American War. On the other hand, for all the text about "anti-imperialists" in the U.S. at this time in the Garraty text, it never explores this phenomena as an enduring concept. Thus the reader is left with the impression that it was only a passing phase in U.S. foreign policy.

Because of these mixed characteristics in each text, it is difficult to clearly declare any of the three texts superior in every way in terms of quality. Consequently, the above criteria based ratings must be considered in conjunction with other factors, including the kinds of topics textbook authors are willing to address and how honestly they do so.

One of the most obvious questions that arises when conducting this type of review, especially if it is about the Latino presence in textbooks, is how much coverage, or how many sentences or pages are enough to consider that this group has been well represented.

While it is possible to make comparisons among textbooks along the quantitative aspects and arrive at relative numbers in terms of sentence counts, there are no easy answers to determining what is enough in an absolute sense. However, if we use the Garraty/Holt textbook as an example, we could calculate that there are about fifteen sentences per page on the average since a full page of text is from 25–27 sentences and the vast majority of pages have shorter texts due to illustrations, photos, etc.

Using a conservative estimate of only fifteen sentences per page divided into the 265 Latino-related sentences in Garraty/Holt would mean that just under 18 pages are dedicated to Latinos in this text. Given that the book is just over 630 pages long, it means that a mere 3% of the book has text focusing on the Latino experience. Without doing the calculations for the other two textbooks, (Davidson/Prentice Hall=376 sentences; Berkin/Scott Foresman=180) it is evident that a few more or fewer percentage points do not alter the overall obvious conclusion that, given their population and historical significance in this nation, Latinos are still grossly underrepresented in these U.S. history textbooks.

From this point of departure, it could be argued that speaking of quality may not be relevant, given that even the best quality writing about Latinos consisted of such a small percentage of the overall narrative that it may not have a considerable impact on students' understanding anyway. Nevertheless, it is important that the five qualitative criteria be considered, measured and met so that what little information about Latinos does appear in textbooks is at least valuable, authentic, and relevant and thus establishes a foundation for more accurate understanding on the part of both students and teachers.

COMPARING TWO TEXTS

In addition to analyzing these three textbooks, I also conducted a contrast-comparison review of two high school textbooks by the same publishers whose earlier texts I had already reviewed, namely Holt R&W and Prentice Hall. Both are being adopted and will be in use in school districts all over the state beginning in Fall, 2003, and for at the least the next ten years.

Boyer, Paul & Stuckey, Sterling. (2003). *The American nation*. Austin, TX: Holt, Rinehart and Winston.

Cayton, Perry, Reed & Winkler. (2003). *America: Pathways to the present*. Englewood Cliffs, NJ: Prentice Hall.

This was not as thorough an analysis as was the above detailed review of the three textbooks. The purposes of this study was simply to compare and contrast in the most general way, how each textbook represents Latinos. In this procedure, the following steps were completed.

1. From chapter headings in the table of contents, do targeted reading of sections which would likely include information about Latinos.
2. Look at the index for terms such as Latino, Hispanic, Mexican American, Puerto Rico, Chicano, etc. and read these sections as well.
3. Review all other chapters and sections of the text to ensure that any Latino related text or graphics have been identified.
4. For each event, individual, concept, etc. noted in the text, document the specific item by name and note it's length.
5. Consider the accuracy, objectivity, and overall quality of each item.
6. Compare and contrast the quantity and quality of the data presented related to Latino/Hispanic topics by each textbook.

Once the data was collected and comparisons were made, a written report was prepared which emphasized the most salient characteristics of each text regarding its Latino representation, and made specific comparisons between both on that regard. This report was then presented orally before the State Board of Education in Austin on September 11, 2002, and typed copies were also distributed to SBOE members present that day.

Comparing Data

The most striking contrast between these texts is the sheer difference in the scope and depth of coverage. The Holt textbook deals with a wide variety of topics related to Mexican Americans. Some include just a few paragraphs, but other topics are described and elaborated on in several pages. Among these are some short biographies as well as discussions of the Mexican vaquero, immigration, migrant workers, and the Zoot Suit Riots.

There is even a seven-page section on the Chicano Movement, (pp. 682–688), which includes quotes, personal testimonials, primary sources, photos, and a map, as well as key personalities, organizations, and events.

In this section, the Holt text also explains more complex concepts including non-violence as practiced by César Chávez and cultural nationalism as espoused by Chicano activists. This particular section in the Holt text on the Chicano Movement serves as a model and established a standard much higher than required by the TEKS of how to thoroughly present an historical topic related to Latinos.

By contrast the Prentice Hall text covers fewer topics related to Latinos, particularly Mexican Americans, and does not enrich its presentation with as many quotes, testimonials, and graphics as does Holt.

Nevertheless, Prentice Hall does dedicate three pages to a section on "Latinos Fight for Change," (pp. 771–773) beginning with the 1960s. Short biographies of Cesar Chavez (p. 773) and Dr. Hector Garcia (p. 703), are included as sidebars. The names of other leaders are briefly mentioned, but there just are not enough words dedicated to the explanation of what they accomplished, what they believed, and the various organizations they founded.

There is also another section on "Mexican Americans" (p. 625—626), which covers the time during and immediately following World War II. Post-war immigration is discussed as are the Bracero program and the Zoot Suit Riots. Yet, what is missing here, which is more evident in the Holt text, is the use of various sources other than text to present a personality or topic.

Overall, the quality of writing is superior in the Holt text, topics are better elaborated on and concepts are explained more fully as well. In terms of the Zoot Suit Riots, the Holt text provides a more thorough historical and economic context to this event than does the Prentice Hall. Besides describing what happened, the Holt text (p. 539) mentions that 300,000 Mexican Americans served in the military, and also the fact that seventeen earned the Congressional Medal of Honor. The Prentice text (p. 626) leaves out this information and also fails to mention, as does the Holt text, that a citizen's committee later determined that racial prejudice had motivated the attacks of soldiers and sailors against Mexican American youths wearing Zoot suits. Holt also includes other relevant information not covered by Prentice Hall namely that the Los Angeles police as well as biased newspaper reports contributed to the attacks and to the general public's prejudice against Zoot suitors.

There are other ways in which the Holt text provides better, more accurate, and complete coverage of Latino topics than does Prentice Hall, but the above serve as the most salient examples. While both textbooks represent a considerable improvement over earlier textbooks on U.S. history, it is clear that one publisher has invested more effort, space and resources to presenting the Latinos' story than the other.

Without having reviewed the other textbooks for U.S. history that were recently adopted, I cannot speak to their quality or quantity in terms of their Latino content; however, the Holt textbook, *The American Nation,* does represent a standard by which others can be compared.

There has been much improvement in the representation of Latinos in textbooks over the last two decades. Yet, the range of Latino diversity, in terms of national origin, racial mixture, cultural heritage, and social class has not been clearly presented in any U.S. history textbook I, and many other investigators, have reviewed. Moreover, the many Latino contributions in the areas of cattle ranching, military service, art, law, literature, music and civil rights, have not been adequately presented in any single textbook.

These two studies could hopefully provide a basis for making concrete suggestions for enhancing, completing, and correcting the information about Latinos that millions of American children and youth will be obtaining from U.S. history textbooks for decades to come.

Chapter Five

Teaching: Making Content Choices

EXPLORING TEACHERS' PERSPECTIVES AND PRACTICES

This study focused on the perspectives, preferences and practices of selected U.S. history teachers in order to identify and explore the factors that influence their choice of content. The ultimate objective was to determine the conditions or obstacles that hinder the teacher's inclusion of Latino or minority-related content into the historical narrative.

Three approaches were used: individual interviews, a focus group, and a content checklist survey. All participants were teachers from the Northside Independent School District, the largest public school district in San Antonio, Texas, encompassing urban, rural and suburban communities, with a racially and economically diverse student body that contains over fifty percent Mexican American students.

San Antonio is a bilingual and bicultural city, with significant historic, economic, and cultural ties to Mexico. Mexican Americans currently comprise about fifty-three percent of the metropolitan population.

Although this Hispanic numerical majority is not typical of most U.S. cities, there are many urban, suburban and increasingly small town areas where a Latino presence is either long-standing or suddenly increasing. Given the particular social and cultural history of San Antonio, as well as the legacy of Chicano/Mexican American political activism and organizing unique to this city, it would be interesting to note the extent to which that Mexican American/Latino/Hispanic heritage is reflected in the history taught in its public schools.

Individual Interviews were conducted with twelve middle and high school U.S. history teachers, and a focus group session was held later with four additional history teachers. Before each individual interview and before the focus group session, each of the sixteen participants filled out a course content checklist containing specific historical items. Each was asked to indicate which items he/she covered in his/her course either a) always, b) sometimes or c) hardly ever/ never. Methods, data and analyses for each of the three approaches are described below.

INDIVIDUAL INTERVIEWS

Purpose and Problem Statements

The purpose of this investigation was to examine the beliefs and perceptions selected U.S. history teachers have regarding the content of their courses. Also examined were some of the factors that impact this content and how these relate to teachers' content choices. Special attention was focused as well on the extent to which, and the context in which, participants mention women, minorities, and especially Latinos (or Hispanics, Mexican-Americans, etc.) regarding their presence in the curriculum.

From the above, three problem statements could be formulated thus:

1) What are the content choices made by these U.S. history teachers?
2) Are these choices influenced by their own beliefs and/or by external factors over which they have little or no control?
3) How do these teachers regard the presence of women, minorities, and especially Latinos in the curriculum content?

Methods, Instruments, and Participants

A series of audiotaped interviews were conducted, supplemented by written notes. Participants included twelve United States history teachers of both genders and from three ethnoracial groups. Some had taught for over twenty years, others barely five, and each had varied types of instructional experiences. They included some who taught the first part of U.S. history (to Reconstruction) at the eighth grade, and others teaching the second part at the high school level.

Entry to Northside I.S.D. and access to participants was not difficult. This was partly facilitated by the fact that for six years I had served as Clinical Supervisor with the University of Northern Iowa for student teachers placed in the this district. After permission was secured from the district's administrative office, the district social studies supervisor sent out a brief memo to all campus social studies coordinators informing them of my investigation. I then made follow up calls to these coordinators and arranged to call and/or e-mail potential participants they identified as current or recent U.S. history teachers who are also outstanding educators.

Most participants were interviewed individually in a private room on their campus, usually after school or during their planning period. One was interviewed at her home. Each signed a standard consent form that, among other things, explained the purpose of the study and clarified his/her role and rights as a participant.

A set of twenty-one initial questions was used with most participants and additional follow-up questions were individualized to probe further into relevant topics (see Appendix C: Interview Questions). These questions related to four general areas: Experience and Background (years of experience and subjects taught); Structural Conditions (administrative support, textbooks, standards, testing); Content Choices (content preferences and issues); and Ultimate Goals (personal satisfaction, what students gain, why teach history).

Working Hypotheses and Data Analysis

Audiotapes, checklists, and notes were reviewed, relevant data was organized and labeled, and specific findings were extracted and documented for analysis and reflection.

Much of this study was exploratory and therefore, no precise hypotheses were being tested, especially given the small sample size. Nevertheless, at least three working hypotheses were posed regarding teachers' perceptions of the structural conditions that affect their choice of content:

1. Most participants will perceive that there is more content to be taught than what time and circumstance permit them to teach.
2. At least one-third of participants will identify specific eras, events or individuals of special interest to them which circumstances do not permit them to teach about well.
3. At least one-half of the participants will mention perceived problems or deficiencies with either the TAAS standardized test (Texas Assessment of Academic Skills), the Texas Essential Knowledge and Skills (TEKS), and/or the adopted textbook.

The analysis of data from each interview was approached in five ways:

1. The three hypotheses were compared to findings.
2. The general pattern of responses to questions about content by all participants was documented.
3. The correlation four participant variables (gender, ethno-race, grade level, experience) have on selected participant responses was noted.

4. The extent to which participants mention women and minorities was documented.
5. The extent to which Latinos are mentioned was determined.

Below are the findings relevant to each one of these five ways of looking at the data followed by a final section summarizing the findings and briefly discussing their implications.

Findings From Interviews

1. The Three Working Hypotheses

Each of the three working hypotheses stated above were assessed according to the data obtained. The first hypothesis was supported with nine of the twelve participants mentioned time constraints as the major obstacle to teaching all the required content. Support for the second hypothesis was abundant with all twelve participants readily volunteering specific areas of personal interest which time constraints prevented them from teaching.

The third hypothesis consisted of three structural issues, (the TAAS, the TEKS, and the textbooks), about which at least one-half the participants would mention problems or deficiencies. This hypothesis was partially supported with six participants having strong critiques of the TAAS test, and the other six mentioning both positive and negative effects of its use. Regarding the TEKS, eight made generally positive statements, while four critiqued the absence of minorities and women. Four made positive statements about the textbooks, while three expressed negative opinions; the other five stated more balanced or neutral views.

The TAAS standardized test was generally viewed as having an influential and negative effect. Half of the participants did voice strong critiques, while the other half made expressed positive and negative effects regarding a test which has gained importance as being the primary instrument for assessment of students, teachers, schools and even school districts statewide. It should be noted that the name of this standardized, criterion-referenced test has recently changed from TAAS to TAKS, (Texas Assessment of Knowledge and Skills), and its importance has further increased with its use as a high-stakes measure.

The TEKS curriculum standards received a positive appraisal from two-thirds of the participants, while one-third critiqued it for the absence of women and minorities. In fact the lack of multicultural content was the only criticism made against the TEKS, although some who made this critique, also agreed that it provided good framework, especially for young and/or inexperienced teachers.

Participants' responses were quite mixed regarding the textbooks being a valuable resource in their teaching. Four made definitely positive statements, three made negative statements and the other five were more neutral or balanced in their assessment of textbooks.

2. General Responses to Content Questions

The questions of greatest relevance to this inquiry have to do with the teachers' choice of content and the specific factors that influence their choices. Among the conditions which impact teachers' instructional decisions is their perception of students' interest in learning history.

Question #6 asks: *What approximate percentages of your classroom students demonstrate an interest in learning history?*

Seven of the twelve participants stated that less than thirty percent are interested in learning history at the beginning of the course. However, five of these seven participants, and two others, also reported that a greater percentage of students eventually became more interested in history by the end of the course. These seven teachers reported that there was an increase from seventeen percent to over fifty percent of students who gained an interest in learning history. Thus, most participants perceived that a significant number of students obtained a more positive attitude towards learning history from taking their course.

Five questions, #12 through #16, focused on the teachers' content preferences. For example, #12 asks: *What eras, events, individuals, developments, etc. do you prefer, or enjoy teaching about the most?*

The responses were quite varied, including such items as:

The Progressive Era, the Great Depression, the Industrial Age, aviation history, Westward Movement, the Gilded Age, colonization period, American Revolution, Manifest Destiny, and the Lewis & Clark Expedition. Wars and their eras, especially World War II, and the Civil War, figured prominently in these favorite choices.

Aside from some personal reasons, i.e., interest in aviation "because his dad was a pilot in WW II," most teachers preferences were related to the pivotal, and transforming significance of the historical event or period. Even most of those that mentioned wars, did so with the understanding that students needed to understand the causes and effects of these conflicts on ordinary people as well as in the battlefield or on the nation as a whole.

Another question, #14, asked participants, *What would you like to teach, cover, include in the curriculum, which, for whatever reasons, you cannot cover in class?* One follow-up question to that was, *What prevents you from covering this material in your class now?*

In response to the first question there was the expected variety of topics ranging from some already mentioned as favorite items in #12, as well as such eras or events as: the 1970s: Nixon & Watergate, Spanish colonization, Vietnam, the Cold War, and environmental history. Three participants mentioned more historical novels, fiction and other literature. Two indicated more hands on and experiential type activities, such as projects and field trips to local sites and museums as something they would like to do. One stated the desire to teach more about ordinary people and how they were impacted by events. Four others mentioned Hispanics, Native Americans, and/or Blacks as well as their heritage and history as topics about which they would teach more if circumstances permitted.

It was also significant to note that, in response to the second question of #14, nine of the twelve participants clearly stated that lack of time was the main reason why they could not teach about topics, eras, or events they would like to. Two indicated that they had not developed the resources or materials necessary, and one mentioned the TAAS test.

The teacher who mentioned the constraining effects of the TAAS test also was one of the respondents who most emphatically stated that he would like to teach more about the influence of minority groups, including the Native American removal, and aspects of Hispanic history.

The other most relevant question to the issue of content choice was the last one in this section, #16, which is really a two-part question: *If you had the power to decide, what overall or specific changes would you make regarding the content covered in your course?* and What's *preventing you from adopting or implementing these changes now?*

Five participants would bring more minorities and women into the curriculum. Two indicated that they would emphasize more Hispanic history and/or heritage and two others would bring Native Americans more to the forefront of the content being taught. One would add more information on women and ethnic groups. Three responded that they would cover early colonization and exploration before the English, since this had been a period characterized by Spanish exploits, and one that had recently been eliminated from the curriculum. Another would change the textbooks and two others suggested structural changes: teaching U.S. history as a three, rather that a two-year course, and teaching the first and second parts of U.S. history consecutively, instead of separating by two or three years.

In response to the second part, seven participants indicated again that time constraints were preventing them from implementing these changes. Three identified existing structures such as the TEKS and the TAAS or the established curriculum scope and sequence as barriers. One identified simply traditional viewpoints as the major obstacle.

3. Participant Variables

Four participant variables were considered in terms of their correlation with participant responses to some questions: years of teaching experience, gender, middle school or high school, and ethnoracial group.

Experience

The first questions related to the teaching background and experience of participants. The diversity in terms of years of experience was clearly marked by a bipolar split. Five of the participants had ten years or more experience teaching U.S. history, whereas the other seven had six years or less. Those same five participants also had fifteen or more years teaching social studies while six of the seven other participants had less than seven years.

Among the five with greatest years of experience, only one expressed any substantial criticism of the textbook. Those with less experience tended to mention more often the biases, omissions or shortcomings of the adopted textbooks.

All but one of the five veterans also had only positive statements to make about the TEKS, whereas most of the teachers with less experience indicated that there were weaknesses in these guidelines. Three teachers, one veteran and two newer teachers, indicated that the major problem with the TEKS was the absence of minorities and women.

Although there was general criticism of the TAAS test, there was a tendency for the veteran teachers to balance their critiques with some positive statement, i.e., more skills are being tested, whereas the newer teachers were more consistently critical of the effects and the construction of the TAAS test.

Gender

In terms of gender, seven of the participants were females of different ages, and representing all three ethnoracial groups in the study. On the textbook question, four of the five males made a disparaging comment. Of the seven females, only one offered a definite critique, two rated textbooks favorably, and four provided mixed reviews.

Between both genders, most respondents agreed that the TEKS provided a sound framework, but they differed somewhat in their assessment of the impact of TAAS on their teaching. None of the participants mentioned anything positive or descriptive about the TAAS without also including some critique of its shortcomings. Yet, four females, a simple majority, made predominantly negative statements about the TAAS, while a majority of males made more balanced statements.

In response to the question on favorite events, eras, etc., four of the five men mentioned multiple wars, and the fifth implied such conflicts by selecting "Manifest Destiny" and the "Westward Expansion." However, of the four women who mentioned war, three listed only one such conflict.

It is also interesting to note that when asked, #13: *What content or elements of the curriculum are not to your liking, preference, or enjoy teaching about the least?* only four participants mentioned battles and/or wars, and all of them were female! One even identified herself as being a pacifist.

Middle School vs. High School

Surprisingly, the views and beliefs history teachers expressed towards the textbooks, TAAS, TEKS were not apparently related to whether they taught at the middle or high school levels. Neither was there any discernible pattern related to the grade level they teach in their responses to the content questions.

Ethnoracial group

Three of the participants were Latinos, (two females), one was an African American female, and the rest were Anglos. In their assessment of the textbook, only one participant of the twelve, the African American, was directly critical of the exclusion of minorities and women. When responding to the question on the TEKS, only three participants, the African American female, the Latino male, and an Anglo female, mentioned that minorities or women were missing.

The four minority participants were more consistently critical of the TAAS test than the Anglos and offered some of most scathing comments. The Latino male: " . . . teaching becomes like trivial pursuit, test items are arbitrary, and teaching any content is hit or miss." The African American female: " . . . it limits creativity and spontaneity of my students. Can we afford to teach what's not going to be on the TAAS?"

Although no participant mentioned minorities or women when asked to name a favorite event, era, or topic, when they discussed why these were of special interest to them, two Latinos and two Anglos made references to minorities. Throughout the interviews, three of the four minority participants mentioned the need for minority inclusion, and two of them, the African American female and the Latino male, also did so consistently.

4. References Made to Women and Minorities

Several unsolicited references or statements were made regarding minorities, or issues of diversity during the interviews. In response to mainly questions about content, on fourteen occasions, eight of the twelve participants mentioned the exclusion of minorities and women from the TEKS or textbooks.

On four occasions, four participants mentioned "women" in the content of the curriculum, two were male, and two were female. Only three participants mentioned either women or minorities when discussing those eras, events, topics, or individuals of special interest to them.

5. References Made to Latinos

Of all twelve interviews, on eight occasions, five participants mentioned "Hispanics" and the need to include them in the curriculum.

Summary and Implications of Findings

Much more data that can be extracted and analyzed from the interviews of this investigation than what was presented above. Nevertheless, we can draw some conclusions and discuss certain implications that are directly relevant to this investigation.

In terms of such structural conditions, most participants were critical of the TAAS test, yet were satisfied with the TEKS standards upon which the TAAS is supposedly based. They had some critiques of the textbooks as well. This implies that U.S. history teachers do not resist standards *per se,* but are critical of how these are assessed with the use of a standardized test.

Although teachers' responses were not related to the grade level of U.S. history they taught, gender did play a role in the content participants most preferred to teach. Females were least interested in battles and wars, while males tended to have more interest in these conflicts. Perhaps this reflects the socialization of males towards violence in our culture, whereby they feel more comfortable discussing the details of battles and bloody struggles than most females do.

The length of experience did also seem to correlate with participants' views on such structural aspects as the TEKS, TAAS and the textbooks. Those with less experience tended to have significantly more criticisms of these official curriculum constraints than did their more experienced veterans. This could mean that younger teachers have been trained to value more flexible, experiential, cooperative, and student-centered approaches to instruction than the older teachers.

The ethnoracial identity of participants did have some correlation with their responses; there was a greater tendency for the four minority participants to make references to the exclusion of women and people of color from the official curriculum. This is not surprising.

However, although most participants did make statements about the exclusion of minorities somewhere during their interviews, and obviously attached some importance to teaching multiculturally, their responses to the checklist reveal that in actual practice, minorities, like women, are consistently left out as will be discussed more fully later.

For now, perhaps the most revealing finding from these checklists filled by individual interviewees, was that of all the names of individuals not covered in their history classes, Latinos are overwhelmingly the most excluded from the curriculum.

The reasons for this may be quite complex, and probably include the fact that many teachers, being products of our public education system, are themselves uninformed or perhaps even ignorant about Latino history and heritage. Another set of reasons, confirmed by this investigation, is that the standards established for curriculum (the TEKS) the vehicle used to teach it (the textbooks), and the instrument used to assess student learning, (the TAAS test), all contribute to the exclusion of Latinos from the history classroom.

The implications of this are clear. Despite the growing numbers and influence of Latinos, and regardless of the pivotal role they have often played as individuals and as groups in our nation's history, they are still being given little or no attention in the history classrooms of these outstanding teachers.

FOCUS GROUP

The primary purpose of this study was to comprehend more completely the factors that influence content choices made by U.S. history teachers. Four other closely related routes of investigation were also pursued in this study: a) to identify the individuals, groups, eras, events, and movements to which teachers dedicate more time and effort in their course, b) to determine the extent to which racial and ethnic minorities are integral to the historical narrative teachers present, c) to measure the relative presence of Latino people and events, and d) to identify the factors which influence the integration of minorities, and the resources and strategies teachers utilize to do so.

Ultimately, this study will contribute to our understanding of how U.S. history teachers engage with the content of their courses, and how these decisions affect the coverage of ethnic and racial minorities, especially Latinos.

Research Questions

The main research question guiding this study was:

> *How do structural and environmental factors influence the extent to which secondary U.S. History teachers in Texas integrate Latinos and other racial/ethnic minorities into the historical narrative taught in the classroom?*

Several sub-questions were also pursued from the data:

Sub-question A:

> *What factors do teachers believe serve to facilitate or frustrate their ability to fully integrate racial and ethnic minorities in their curriculum?*

Sub-questions B:

> *To what extent do history teachers regard Latinos/Hispanics as significant to the historical narrative they present?*
>
> > *a. How much time do they spend on Latino topics?*
> >
> > *b. What Latino individuals, groups and related events do they cover?*
> >
> > *c. Why do they value this inclusion or not?*
> >
> > *d. Do they feel they are doing an adequate job?*

Sub-questions C:

> *To what extent do teachers believe in the importance of integrating racial and ethnic minorities into the content they cover?*
>
> > *a. Why do they value this or not?*
> >
> > *b. Do they feel they are doing an adequate job?*

We might not have been able to answer every question or set of questions completely from the data generated; however, a special attempt was made to design the wording of the focus group questions and to ask follow-up questions in order to cover all the identified topics and sub-topics.

Many of the questions used for this focus group were similar to those used for the individual interview. Please refer to Appendix D: Focus Group Questions to access the questions planned as well as those actually used.

Focus Group Design

Data was gathered by means of a focus group consisting of four history teachers of various backgrounds from the Northside I.S.D. in San Antonio, Texas.

Focus groups offer certain advantages that could enhance the qualitative value of the data generated. In addition to simply finding responses to the research questions, this study also attempted to understand where there is consensus versus controversy, if any, among history teachers regarding critical factors which impact their instructional content and approach.

Using focus groups also allowed for interaction among participants and thus stimulated the flow of ideas, opinions, and perspectives in a friendly, collegial setting. In comparing focus groups to individual interviews, Madriz (2000) states that " . . . the clear advantage of focus groups is that they make it possible for researchers to observe the interactive processes occurring among participants" (p. 836).

This could provide an opportunity for authentic expression to occur which would contain a rich collection of data ranging from simple complaints and frustrations to more fundamental issues of pedagogy or ideology. In a stimulating environment, perhaps spontaneous expressions of profound insight as well as obvious errors of fact might be captured. All of these had significance and were recorded.

Attempting to systematize the myriad of choices researchers make when using focus groups, Fern clarifies the process by indicating that there are " . . . three different research purposes, three moderating styles, three group sizes and three gender or minority mixes to choose from" (Fern, 2001, p. 1).

In terms of research purposes, he discusses how focus group research can be adopted for three different research tasks: exploratory, experiential, and clinical, and how each of the three can be used to test or generate theory or to effect more practical applications.

Given the definitions Fern utilizes, the experiential type focus group was probably the best approach for this study. In the experiential approach, the researcher attempts to "draw out shared life experiences rather than those that are unique or unshared" (Ibid, 8). Fern also states that in terms of theory, application of experiential focus groups is most useful for triangulation (comparing results across different methods), and confirmation (comparing gathered information with the researcher's prior beliefs)(Ibid). Clearly, since this effort is based on previously conducted individual interviews which yielded specific results, the experiential approach would better serve the objective of achieving triangulation by comparing the results of this focus group with the individual interviews.

The procedure consisted of having the four U.S. history teachers gathered in a comfortable room. Seating was arranged around one table, so as to maximize face-to-face interaction among participants. The moderator sat close to or among the participants.

As participants walked in, the moderator and two assistants welcomed them with refreshments, asked each to sign in, fill out the content checklist, and read over a letter of intent that explained the purpose of the study and clarified the conditions of their participation and legal rights. Please refer to Appendix E: Letter of Intent for a copy of this letter.

Once all participants had gathered, and after a few introductions, the moderator began the discussion, using prompts generated from the six research questions. The session lasted close to ninety minutes, and was audio taped. Some note taking was also done. The audiotaped session was later transcribed and the notes typed out for analysis.

Participants and Sampling

It was important to the study that there be some gender, ethnic, racial, and professional diversity among participants. In addition to being secondary U.S. history teachers, all participants were to be from schools with a student population that is at least one-third Latino or Hispanic.

Other specific criteria for selecting participants included teachers who a) have taught U.S. history for at least two years; b) have taught at least two years in Texas public schools; and c) are certified to teach U.S. history in Texas. Although the original intent was to recruit at least two focus groups circumstances did not permit.

Since circumstances did not permit a strict random selection of participants we contacted the social studies supervisor in each campus to generate interest and obtain participants. Participants were selected on the basis of their interest and availability from a list provided by Northside ISD. As stated above this district encompasses a wide variety of ethnoracial groups and socioeconomic lifestyles, with Latinos comprising a majority of the student body. Given the student demographics, U.S. history teachers from this district would likely have had considerable contact with Latino students as well as with Latino professional colleagues.

Given that the dynamics of smaller groups are considerably different than those in larger ones, Morgan states that the usual practice is to use "moderate sized" groups of six to ten (1988, 43). I planned for six participants, of both genders, but unfortunately only four were present, all males but of diverse ethnoracial background and years of experience.

I was not too concerned about not doing random sampling because of the exploratory nature of our investigation. Krueger clarifies that focus group researchers use "purposeful" sampling whereby participants are selected based on the purpose of the study. However, due to unforeseen circumstances, this investigation could not proceed to select participants in the manner suggested by Krueger: " . . . the researcher often assembles a pool of potential participants and then selects randomly from within this pool of qualified individuals. This level of randomization is regularly done, and it helps minimize selection bias" (Kruger, 1998, p. 71).

Data Collection

The audiotape, and the transcript generated from it, served as the major vehicle for data collection and preservation. The moderator also took notes after the session to document certain overall aspects of the session not easily perceived from a detailed transcription. Notes taken by a colleague during the session were also typed out for review and analysis.

A technician using a soundboard with individual microphones for each participant assisted me. Another assistant took rudimentary notes on who was speaking and topics discussed so that the order in which participants spoke was in correct sequence. The note-taking assistant and I debriefed following the interview, identifying some of the major issues generated in the discussion and also characterizing the general mood of participants as well as the climate of the discussion.

According to Krueger (1998), there are several steps that researchers should take in the collection of data so as to ensure that the subsequent analysis is systematic. He identifies six specific steps which this research effort attempted to complete, as summarized below:

1. Sequencing of the questions to allow maximum participant insight
2. Sound process for capturing and handling data
3. Proper coding of data, specifically the use of axial coding
4. Participant verification of data collected
5. Debriefing between moderator and assistant moderator immediately after the focus group
6. Sharing both preliminary and later reports with participants and stake holders (pp. 10–11)

Approach to Data Analysis

According to Morgan (1988), there are two basic approaches to analyzing focus group data: the systematic coding via content analysis, and the essentially qualitative ethnographic summary. This study attempted to use both approaches, relying more on the coding and analysis of the content as a foundation. Morgan asserts that: "These are not, however, conflicting means of analysis, and there is generally an additional strength that comes from combining the two" (Morgan, 1988, p. 64).

Thus, the analysis *per se* would involve reviewing and coding the transcripts first, in light of the research questions being considered. Then a more ethnographic approach would be used to provide a synthesis of groups' characteristics and responses as a whole. Quotes from participants that either articulates a consensus view or which provide a unique perspective were selected and considered. They serve to expand our understanding of teachers' responses further.

In a chapter titled, "The Analysis Process," Krueger provides a detailed step-by-step overview of the analytical process. With a few exceptions, i.e. "Discuss options with sponsor," this study intended to adhere to most of the steps he outlines, dealing with a comprehensive set of factors including note-taking, recording, and labeling notes and tapes (1988, pp. 41–52).

Validity and Generalizability

The search for consensus among participants across diverse backgrounds was one aspect of attempting to establish validity in this study. In addition, previous research results from the study of individual interviews, and from other research on history teachers, also served as sources of validation for the results and process of this investigation. This would create opportunities to use triangulation.

In discussing the advantages of linking focus groups with individual interviewing, Morgan states that " . . . there are reasons to conduct focus groups before and after individual interviews, and even circumstances in which one would want to alternate back and forth between the two methods" (1988, p. 31).

In this effort, the initial study of individual interviews with U.S. history teachers helped confirm any findings regarding emerging themes and influential factors.

Given the nature and process of conducting focus groups, this study does not attempt to ensure generalizability, since the participants were a rather select group not chosen by pure randomization. Krueger suggests, however, the concept of "transferability," whereby the receiver of the study can decide if the methods, procedures, and participants are relevant, the extent to which this study's findings can transfer to another environment (1998, pp. 69–70).

Findings From the Focus Group

A few questions were deleted and others added in the actual course of the focus group interview. Please refer to Appendix D to access the questions planned as well as those actually used.

The approximately ninety minute session was audiotaped and later transcribed, resulting in thirty-eight pages of text.

During the entire discussion the climate was cordial, friendly, open, comfortable, and at times quite humorous. In keeping with the overall climate, the participants were upbeat, positive, and talkative.

These positive conditions facilitated our generating honest and authentic dialogue and were mostly a reflection of the personalities and dispositions of the four participants. We would also like to believe that these dynamics were also facilitated by our deliberate effort to reflect on and implement a certain approach to this effort; that is, to define the role of the moderator and have the assistants engage in and also support that role.

Thus, in addition to providing participants with ample refreshments and a modest $30 gift certificate to Barnes & Noble, we agreed upon six specific objectives for the moderator's role:

1. set a friendly, cordial, respectful and professional climate
2. ask interesting and stimulating questions
3. encourage openness, honesty and authenticity from participants
4. pursue participant-generated themes with probing questions
5. demonstrate appreciation for and valuing of all opinions
6. encourage maximum participation from all

Based on our observations, and on a close reading of the transcript, I could confidently say that for the most part, these objectives were achieved, admittedly in no small measure due also to the characteristics of the participants themselves.

The data was analyzed and is presented below from the perspective of five major interrelated themes which helped me better understand the perspectives and preferences of the participants. The five themes are:

1. *Content Preferences:* specific eras, events, persons, etc. of greatest interest to participants and their students.
2. *Structural Conditions:* the Four Ts: TAKS standardized test, TEKS curriculum standards, Textbooks officially adopted for use, and Time to teach all the required and desired content. All

four factors impose conditions, which influence content choice and methods.

3. *Other Factors, Issues, and Problems:* factors other than the 4 Ts, as identified by participants themselves.

4. *Recommendations and Solutions:* suggestions by participants for overall improvement and for specific practices that work well.

5. *Coverage of Racial & Ethnic Minorities:* the extent to which women and minorities are part of the narrative and the conditions or factors that facilitate or restrict their inclusion.

Although each major theme would naturally be associated with a specific set of questions, it was important to note that some questions did generate discussions which engaged two or more themes. Please note that whereas the interview participants had referred to the standardized test as the TAAS, it was referred to as the TAKS test by focus group participants since it had recently been renamed.

Each of the five will be discussed below using the data from both the transcript and tape, considering that the spoken word more accurately conveys a sense of emotion and emphasis not always evident from the transcribed text. In addition to identifying the responses to theme-related questions, I also noted the extent to which particular responses or views generated convergence (agreement or consensus) or divergence (contradiction or variety) among the participants. On some occasions I may also have identified the particular participant by race or ethnicity, when the issues in discussion related to these factors.

Overall, this data presentation and analysis paid special attention whenever appropriate, to the relevance participant responses have to the coverage of women, minorities, and particularly Latinos in the content of the U.S. history course.

1. Content Preferences

As with the individual interviews, there was wide divergence among participants regarding their response to the first question: *What eras, events, individuals, developments, etc. do you prefer, or enjoy teaching about the most? Why?*

Responses ranged from "modern history" with a focus on "space exploration" to the "young years of the republic" with an emphasis on the founding documents. Other favored content included long eras involving a wide range of years, for example, "Civil War to the present" or somewhere shorter ranges: from "World War I . . . to the Vietnam War" or the "immediate past" or the "antebellum period."

In two instances in the context of favored content, statements with relevance to race or ethnicity were made, both related to the African American experience. One of the two Anglo teachers mentioned the "Civil Rights Movement" in the context of expressing a preference for contemporary history.

While claiming greater interest in the "Civil War to the present" the African American teacher also mentioned by name the "Antebellum Period, post Civil War, and Reconstruction Era," all periods with significant African American presence and historical role.

In addition to a divergence of content preferences, there was some very focused attention on the "Gilded Age" (early 19th to early 20th centuries), by way of direct disagreement about its historical value and interest. The discussion was all very well mannered and even humorous at times, but it was perhaps one of the few times in the entire session when participants openly expressed opposing viewpoints, and did so with extended arguments imbedded within their responses to several questions.

Question #3: *What would you like to teach, cover, include in the curriculum, which, for whatever reasons, you cannot cover in class?* also elicited a wide range of responses:

- the entertainment aspect of social history, i.e., Elvis, Beatles, Puff Daddy
- the immigrant experience and their problems, and race relations
- the Gilded Age and its issues and problems via social history
- student selected biographies, critical thinking, and technology activities

Despite the apparent diversity of responses, there was openly stated preference for teaching "social history," a term participants used repeatedly, especially as it relates closely to students' interest as well as their own. One participant, the African American, even identified himself as more of a "social historian" both by deliberate choice and academic preparation.

There were other references to content, and even more so, content related to women and ethnoracial minorities in the context of discussions about structural conditions and student characteristics. These are covered below in the contexts in which they are mentioned.

In response to the first three questions related to reasons why participants favored or disfavored particular content, there was more general agreement along key criterion such as the significance of an historical era or event, the relevance it has for today, and the interest it stimulates among students. In terms of contemporary relevance and student interest, there was strong consensus that students were more stimulated by more modern history to which they could relate with greater ease by making connections with their own lives.

2. Structural Conditions: The Four Ts

There was much discussion about: 1. the TAKS standardized test, 2. the TEKS curriculum standards, 3. adopted textbooks, and 4. Time, or the lack of it to cover the required, let alone the desired curriculum. All four are conditions over which U.S. history teachers have little or no control.

In fact, before the planned questions about these four factors were asked, they had emerged from the participants own responses, beginning with question #3 regarding content they would like to cover but cannot for whatever reasons.

The first statement, made by the self-described "social historian" in the group was about textbooks: " . . . but I find that the texts are so politically based . . . that it just drives us to just teach who the Presidents are. . . ."

The lack of time was also mentioned by another participant who also identified the TAKS test as a limiting factor in response to question #3. Sensing agreement in the group, I interjected a probing question, #3P, which inquired about the effect of the TAKS test: *What effect will the TAKS state standardized test have on the curriculum content and your teaching?*

Most responses about the effects of TAKS were negative. One participant summarized much of the discussion and consensus with the following statement: " . . . we are going more towards trivia style questions as opposed to critical or analytical thinking skills that will help them not just be good at doing history, but good students period . . ."

The discussion about TAKS and TEKS, although not specifically solicited, continued as a response to question #4: *What prevents you from covering the material or engaging in the activities you would like in your class?*

The TEKS standards, to which teachers are "obligated" as district employees to follow, were first mentioned as a limiting factor. Another participant mentioned the TAKS, and its predecessor TAAS test, as being "very structured and very limiting on what we could teach . . ." He also mentioned the numerous TEKS biographies as well as the over twenty pages of glossary terms also under the TEKS that students had to know. All this material was "very much proscribed" and it served to ready students for a forty question test, in which much of what they had covered wasn't even mentioned.

There was much convergence about the negative effects of TAKS; one participant even conceded that, "I'm not totally against standardized testing, but I think the TAKS is hurting . . ." The "social historian" expressed his view this way:

> . . . (with) the TAKS test, they want (students) to memorize facts, facts, facts . . . and I don't agree that that's an accurate view of history . . . I think its very limiting to students because it doesn't give them an opportunity to start thinking about history . . .

The TAKS test was also mentioned as a "slow down device," in the context of being an obstacle to making innovative changes in teaching.

There was one positive mention of the TAKS test by a participant in the sense that with it, social studies now has more accountability, as do math and English, and therefore more attention is given to this formerly neglected subject.

When we arrived at the actual planned question about the TAKS, #10: *What effect does the TAKS test have on your teaching of U.S. history?* I decided to ask it anyway, sensing that there were still more thoughts participants had not yet expressed about its effects and implications.

Two respondents were quite clear in their assessment of the effects of TAKS. One participant, teaching at the middle school level stated that

> . . . there's this tremendous amount of pressure revolving around the TAKS . . . Last year, 2001–02 was the first year that history actually counted (in terms of) a school's recognized status . . . it affects everything, the pressure to perform well on it.

Another participant, who put on his "department coordinator's hat" to respond to this question, enumerated four "effects of the standardized tests,"

1. training for teachers . . . you're going to have to know how to analyze . . . that single sheet of data coming back from the student.
2. it changes the scope and sequence" (changing which high school year U.S. history is taught in order to coincide with the TAKS)
3. accountability of the teacher . . . and social studies teachers have never faced that kind of accountability.
4. allocation of resources, both financially and personnel . . . I've already had discussions (about) which teacher to put in what class . . . we need high TAKS scores, and they can deliver them.

When I asked him to summarize his overall assessment of these combined effects, he responded quickly and unequivocally: "I see them as negative because they distract from what good teaching is . . ."

When asked question #9 about the TEKS, the curriculum guidelines that set the standards for TAKS, teacher training and classroom teaching, *Do the TEKS provide a sound framework for the teaching of U.S. history?* participants expressed more divergent views.

One participant responded with a simple, "I'm going to say no," and followed up by clarifying that although TEKS may now provide a sound framework, "I believe in 3, 4, 5 years from now they will not . . . And the reason is that they're going towards people, places, events, rather than cause, effect, linkages, and . . . the WHY of history . . ."

Another participant clearly stated that

> As of right now, I do like the TEKS. I do think they're fairly high order thinking . . . TEKS helps let students know that there's a possibility this might be on the test . . . and they feel that it's important . . . I would like a little; bit more flexibility, but at least it can give us a framework.

The middle school teacher also gave TEKS a positive assessment: " . . . TEKS are OK at the middle school level . . . they are thorough and have a balance of knowledge and skills, and they're both presented well . . ."

In terms of textbooks, there were two specific questions about this structural factor, over which teachers, at least in Northside I.S.D., do have some measure of control in that they have opportunities to either serve on a textbook committee, as one of our participants did, or to at least cast a vote on which publisher's textbook to adopt. The first question was #8 A: *To what extent do the required or adopted textbooks serve as a valuable resource in your teaching?*

There was widespread agreement on two points. One was that the textbooks themselves are limiting or deficient in some way:

> . . . I really didn't rely on the book, because I found it too structured, and dumbed down . . . basically to the lowest common denominator . . . 'Any teacher could' was the phrase that you would hear the representatives say. Actually 'anybody could.' Someone could just walk in, grab a teacher edition and then teach the class, according to publishers . . .

On this point, another participant added that:

> . . . I've seen textbooks come and go over the years . . . there were shortcomings all along . . . I was rarely impressed . . . there's no textbook that

teachers can utilize 100% of the time. It's supplementary . . . there's a
lot of other things out there . . .

Those "other things" were the central item of the participants' second
general point of agreement regarding textbooks. That is, it's not the textbooks *per se* that are viewed as valuable, but rather the "ancillary materials," namely, the maps, charts, videos, websites, software,
supplementary readings, and other resources which accompany the pur-
chase of textbooks.

Even the most ardent textbook critic extolled the useful resources
contained in the software that came with the textbooks, including test gen-
erators and map reading charts, all "very nicely done." "I think this latest
round of adoption has changed my opinion as to what role a book will play
. . . the book, not much . . . the ancillaries, specifically the software, a lot."

One participant, who for the first time had experienced a round of textbook adoption, recalls being directly told by his supervisors, "Don't look at
. . ." or consider the ancillary materials. "Don't let that be a part of my judgment (they told me), but that was really a big part of my judgment."

In response to the second question, #8B, about textbook content,
*How about the content of the textbook itself . . . What's your opinion
about the content, and how effectively that content is covered?* there was
also considerable convergence of opinion, especially in terms of the usual
deficiencies often expressed about textbooks. The first respondent, the
"social historian," stated that

> . . . it was a limited social perspective on history being presented . . .
> Telling of history from one perspective . . . not dealing with historical
> debates, the fact that historians themselves disagree as to what really
> happened, or what was the cause, or effect, or what have you . . . I find
> it just one dimensional, myopic, and very limiting . . .

Another participant agreed: "Why can't they put an opposing viewpoint
section in that book, you know, what would that hurt?" The "social historian" later characterized textbooks as providing " . . . a sound byte presentation of history . . . no substantive discussion of people outside of the
mainstream . . . they're thrown in or added for color or spice . . . They're
not part of the text of the book . . ." And when I asked him to identify who
"they" were, he responded:

> . . . we're talking about minorities, we're talking about Native Americans
> . . . (having) no agency in history . . . Why is it that Chief Joseph is not

presented as a primary source? What are his thoughts on what's going on, as opposed to just . . . 'They chased him, and ran him down,' and that's it . . . You will see in the history textbook his picture, and it gives a little picture, and then they've covered minorities in history. And so it's the sound byte, the tokenist way, or approach (to history). . . . they're trying to throw in minorities . . . and they give them no agency in history.

It is interesting to note that in this entire discussion of structural factors, and even on other themes, the above was the most extended statement any participant ever made about racial or ethnic minorities in the teaching of history. It was made by the African American teacher who had already self-identified as the "social historian."

3. Other Factors, Issues, Problems

A variety of other issues were generated by the discussion, all of these identified as having an impact on the choice of content and its mode of presentation. Foremost among these were student characteristics, especially related to interest and skill levels. Also given much attention was the general time constraints or the sheer lack of time to cover all the required content.

Closely related to the issue of time is the wide consensus expressed by participants affirming the advantages of block scheduling (with 90 minutes of instruction per period), over the traditional daily schedule that consists of seven or eight 50 to 55-minute class periods.

In terms of student characteristics, one respondent, in response to question #6 shared:

But I think the biggest problem I have is the students come in way below grade level. And I think critical thinking is good, but I'm also a believer in building a foundation before you build the roof . . . and I think that's the most critical problem that we're under is some of those kids, whether through social promotion, or whatever, are coming in under grade level, and it's vastly affecting what we are going to teach.

Later on in the session, I asked a direct planned question, #11: *How does the capacity, interest level, or other characteristics of your students influence your choice of content?*

The first response to that was from a participant who enthusiastically extolled the importance of making instruction interesting to students, especially because " . . . in social studies . . . we realize that it's quite possible we have the lowest student interest of any subject in high school."

And when I challenged him by mentioning math as a low interest subject, he agreed but added that

> Can you think of a subject that has more possibilities than history? Think about it . . . we can do a lot. There's a lot of flexibility. You know with math, there's only so many times you can bring in pizza, and say, 'Hey, let's do fractions!' Eventually you're going to get bored with that. Whereas with history you got role-plays, and simulations, you can do games, you can access primary sources . . .

Providing students with choices as a way of sparking interest, was a practice that was widely supported by all participants. One put it this way: " . . . and that's where the enthusiasm has got to come in with the students . . . let them choose, its their education, not yours."

Another reinforced the importance of addressing student interest, but added that it had to be balanced with curriculum content:

> I try to balance student influence and curriculum to whatever makes them laugh, or whatever entertains them . . . I struggle with that because there are certain things I want to impart to them . . . but the means by which they're introduced to it . . . I could care less.

Another participant summed up his view of student characteristics with two concepts: "the depth of learning," and the "breadth of information." To describe depth of learning he used a metaphor of "pushing a student up a mountainside," and explained that " . . . the idea is to get them up to the extent of their ability, let them see that there's far more out there, and push'em."

Breadth of information was exemplified by a methodology: " . . . teach (students) how to set up a cause-effect relationship, and then apply that to anything, across time . . . And if they can manage that, and most of them can, they're going to do a good job."

Student interest also connected with time restrictions, the one other factor participants identified as having a significant influence on what and how they teach. For this participant, it had to do with the pace and the depth at which he covered certain content. Speaking of student interest, he agreed that

> . . . it is a big influence because it dictates how fast we go or how slow we go. I don't slow down because it's an area that I like. I usually slow down because it's an area that they have all those questions in. (For

example) We spent a lot of time on socialism in America, because that is something they have never dealt with . . . It wasn't something that I really wanted to focus on . . . but they wanted to focus in on it.

Most participants had, at various points in our discussion, identified time restrictions as causing limitations on what content was covered, how and to what extent. At one point, there was quite an interest in discussing the pros and cons of "block scheduling."

After one participant had raised the issue in the context of what were the obstacles hindering innovation, I decided to ask others in what became question #7P: *What are the effects or advantages and disadvantages of block scheduling?*

All four participants registered their opinion detailing the obvious advantages of block scheduling, none mentioned any disadvantages. There was perhaps as much consensus on this point as on any other in this discussion. One participant made the case quite cogently:

I just think it's imperative that you have that time, especially with an issue, (or) when you talk about skills, or about abstract things to students, you need to be there to . . . not necessarily direct them, but to let them bounce things off of you . . . And I just don't think in fifty minutes, that's something that could be done . . . And so much of my class is discussion based, that if I didn't have fifty minutes of just discussion, or manipulation of materials . . . I'd be wasting my time.

4. Recommendations and Solutions

On several occasions, with or without prompting questions, participants expressed clear ideas about what works, what doesn't, and what can be done to resolve certain problems. Perhaps some of the boldest recommendations from participants came in response to question #6, which of course, fulfilled the very intent of the question: *If you had the power to decide, what overall or specific changes would you make regarding the content covered in your course?*

One participant stressed the importance of methodology and skills development over covering specific content in teaching history:

There's a reason we have encyclopedias . . . so we will not have to remember all of that stuff . . . it's more important to be able to teach a student how to retrieve the data they want, how to manipulate it, and how to build a new structure with the components.

He, an Anglo male, would in fact, do away with curriculum content as we know it:

> I would throw out all the Dead White Guys, all the dates, all the bat-
> tles, and I would bring in a curriculum that stresses the ability to ana-
> lyze, to synthesize, evaluate, think critically, and problem solve. And
> (also the ability) to set up a research project and do all those things that
> they will be doing throughout their lives . . . Not playing jeopardy.

Another participant wanted to instruct students to become: " . . . more critical thinkers . . . to be able to present an issue, a position, and then have
them really look at all the sides of it."

Followed by loud laughter, one participant exclaimed, "I have a God
complex" and then he explained that " . . . in my infinite wisdom, and this
vast experience . . . I have a problem with periodization."

Then he went on to suggest a fundamental change that would indeed
seem to require divine intervention, given the resources involved, which is,
adding a third U.S. history class. He would divide history up to the eigh-
teenth century in the first course, deal with the nineteenth in the second,
and then have an entire third course for the twentieth century until today.
That would, in his opinion, allow time for all the kinds of projects, and
innovative, student-centered approaches that most participants had
unequivocally identified as characteristics of good history teaching. In
terms of content, this participant also shared his thoughts about the "Dead
White Guys" as mentioned by another colleague, and made another linkage
between content and the structural limitations of time:

> . . . Dead White Guys . . . They are significant, they're important . . .
> however, I think they've been overemphasized because of time restric-
> tions that we've been in. Because we got to give them what we believe
> are the hotspots of history, and we got to do this on the quick."

5. Coverage of Racial & Ethnic Minorities

Upon reviewing participants' responses overall, and more specifically in the
context of the four themes explored, it is clear that on several occasions references were made to the coverage of women and minorities. In the
process, several obstacles that restrict opportunities to bring in this content
and perspective were identified and included the three Ts, TEKS, TAKS and
textbooks, as well as the ever-present factor of time. Even student interest
seemed to play a role.

In order to ensure complete discussion on this topic, naturally of special interest to this investigation, we asked this final question, #16: *What is it that hinders or helps your ability to adequately cover the role of racial and ethnic minorities in the teaching of U.S. history?*

All four participants responded to this question, and their responses echoed closely other statements which had been made earlier in the discussion. The first participant to respond mentioned time restrictions, but especially textbooks as hindering factors: " . . . it would be time constraints and the pressures of covering your content. And the textbook, in terms of racial and ethnic minorities, just glosses over. Many events and many important things are left out."

Another participant admitted having relatively few opportunities to gain the knowledge about racial and ethnic minorities, even from his college or university training. Not having this was an obstacle: "It's not YOUR curriculum, so if you don't have that background knowledge, if you don't have that comfort zone, I think a lot of teachers have trepidation introducing it in their class."

One participant informed us that in his entire high school and college experience, speaking of his teachers and professors, " . . . not one of them was anybody other than a White guy, specifically in my history classes. I don't think I ever had a minority person who was a teacher . . . not one."

Then he shared his view that " . . . it is entirely possible to teach U.S. history from a minority point of view . . . Strictly . . . All you have to do is decide which minority you want to talk about . . . Because when Europeans first came here, *they* were minorities."

After his comments generated some general laughter, he mentioned two major obstacles to the coverage of minorities: the lack of proper teacher training or continuing education for teachers, and textbook content. To make his point about textbooks he used an old *Men and Nations* book, and after commenting on the chauvinistic nature of the title itself, he informed us that of the forty plus chapters in this world history book, only four were about "non-European, non-U.S. history."

The fourth participant responded to this question by decrying the influence of what he called "traditionalists" under whose direction, "the contributions of the bottom of society are undervalued in the context of the foundation of history . . ."

According to this respondent, no real progress will be made in addressing what another participant called "a lot of inertia," "until we overcome the devaluing of those individuals, whether it's some ethnic minority, racial minority or gender type of thing . . ."

He also agreed that teacher training is part of the problem: "I was in graduate school before I could actually begin to look at and evaluate gender issues, class issues, racial issues on that level because otherwise it was still with, you know, the Dead White Guys."

In the course of his final statements, other participants also interjected "testing" and "textbooks," once again, as having, like did teacher training, a limiting or restricting influence on their ability to teach about racial and ethnic minorities.

One very significant observation must be made, however, regarding the coverage of Latinos throughout this focus group session. With all the discussion that emerged about ethnoracial minorities, again by direct or indirect prompting, *not once was the term "Latino" "Hispanic" "Mexican American" or any other such term ever mentioned by any participant in this entire wide-ranging discussion.* And although the names of Chief Joseph, Booker T. Washington, and W.E.B. DuBois were specifically mentioned, *not once was the name of any specific Latino individual uttered throughout the entire discussion.*

In fact, it had been our intent *not* to use any term for Latino groups or individuals by name in the questioning, and to only do so after any one of the participants had done so. Significantly, that opportunity never arose.

That this should happen is quite surprising, when it was obvious that the moderator, two assistants, and one of the four participants were Latinos; that is, of the seven people in the room, four were Latinos. It is also important to note that this discussion occurred in San Antonio, Texas, a city and state more infused with Latino influence than most others in the nation and in the largest urban-suburban school district in town, Northside I.S.D., wherein over half the student population is Latino.

This raises a strong possibility that perhaps there was deliberate avoidance operating as an underlying norm among participants. This contrasts directly with the fact that significant Latino-related terms and names were mentioned and discussed by several U.S. history teachers involved in the companion study, the individual interviews.

Whatever can be speculated about the reasons for this phenomena of exclusion, it is perhaps useful to posit that perhaps Latinos are so absent from the standard curriculum, when compared to African Americans and American Indians, that there exists in the minds of teachers, even those who are aware of minority underrepresentation, a clear disconnect between U.S. history and the Latino experience.

That Latinos should be absent by direct reference from this discussion wherein references were made about not only African Americans and American Indians, but "Asians" as well, perhaps speaks to the very thoroughness with which Latinos are excluded or underrepresented from every important vehicle for the teaching of U.S. history.

COURSE CONTENT CHECKLISTS

Each of the sixteen participants filled out either one of two checklists, which consisted of a collection of individuals, concepts, eras, or documents which are relevant to either the eighth grade or high school U.S. history course. About 85% to 90% of items on both checklists were taken directly from the state official curriculum guidelines, the Texas Essential Knowledge and Skills (TEKS). The other items focused on historically significant women and/or minority leaders, groups or relevant events not mentioned in the TEKS.

Participants were directed to mark "A" for those items always taught, "B" for those sometimes covered, and "C" for those never taught. For a copy of each checklist, please refer to Appendix F: Middle School Checklist and Appendix G: High School Checklist.

It is important to note that of the individuals mentioned on both checklists, Anglo males dominate the list, as is reflected in the TEKS. The high school checklist, for example, has forty-two individuals identified by name, five are African American, six are Latinos, four are Anglo women, and twenty-seven are Anglo males.

The procedure was to focus on the items marked "C," those never or hardly ever taught about or covered, according to the respondent, in his/her course. Although the analysis of A or B marked items may be of secondary interest, our primary focus was to determine which specific individuals, organizations, events, or concepts are consistently excluded.

Focusing on what is excluded or hardly ever taught permits us to observe patterns in teachers' decision making regarding content coverage as well as to determine what group or groups are most excluded and whether or not this exclusion occurs consistently by all or most participants.

Checklists from Individual Interviews

As mentioned above participants had been asked to fill out a course content checklist with names of individuals, events, groups, documents, etc., the vast majority of which, (85%-90%) were taken directly from the TEKS guidelines.

From the checklists, a total of forty-five items were marked as "C" by participants. Of these, the overwhelming majority, thirty-five of them, were minorities or women. Thus, when it comes to having to leave something out, for whatever reasons, minority individuals and groups, as well as women are excluded from the curriculum. The three organizations on the list of items least covered by participants were: The National Organization of Women (NOW), the Mexican American Legal Defense and Education Fund (MALDEF), and the League of United Latin American Citizens (LULAC).

From the checklists, it is also interesting to note that of the fourteen names of individuals which were marked "C" three or more times, two were African American males: Alex Hailey, and Benjamin Benneker. What is especially revealing is that of these fourteen most excluded names, twelve were Latinos! They include such historical figures as Bernardo de Galvez, David G. Farragut, Father Junipero Serra, Ponce de Leon, Hernán Cortez, Henry B. Gonzalez, William C. Velasquez, and Benito Juarez.

Checklists from Focus Group Participants

Before beginning the focus group session, as the four participants came into the room and were greeted, each was asked to fill out the same course content checklist, as had the individual interviewees. One participant filled out the middle school checklist; three filled the high school one.

Analyzing these responses again from the perspective of what was usually left out, or "not covered," namely items marked C, the results were consistent with those from individual interviewees. Looking at all four checklists, I counted thirty-seven items in total marked C for the category of "Individuals, Groups and Organizations." The majority of those, twenty items, were of Latino individuals (18) or organizations (2). The organizations least covered by focus group participants were the same as ones also excluded by the individual interviewees, namely LULAC, MALDEF and NOW.

For the "Eras and Events" section, there were only four Cs given, evidently most items in this category were well covered. However, predictably, of the four events not covered, one was the "Indian Wars and Removal," and two were Latino-related, namely the "Chicano Movement" and the "Cuban Revolution."

The results of both sets of course content checklists only confirm two recurring patterns of exclusion already noted in TEKS, textbooks, and teaching: 1) that women and minorities are given less attention and coverage and 2) that among ethnoracial minorities, Latinos are the most disproportionately underrepresented in the teaching of U.S. history.

It is also important to note that this occurs even in the classrooms of most of these sixteen outstanding teachers, selected for their instructional excellence and innovative approaches. What we could expect in terms of Latino coverage from less dedicated or prepared teachers, is a difficult question to answer, but one that needs to be considered.

Chapter Six

Testimony: A Battle for the Text

PUBLIC TESTIMONY REGARDING U.S. HISTORY TEXTBOOKS

The textbook adoption process in Texas is a complex, multiyear project involving writing committees, public hearings, and written testimony as the major vehicles for citizen involvement.

The significance of this component study derives from the fact that it focused on the public testimony process, one of the most powerful influences on decisions regarding textbook adoption in Texas, as it is in California and other states. Textbook testimony is as much a political as it is a pedagogical arena for competing worldviews as to what constitutes accuracy and comprehensiveness in textbooks for history and social studies. Thus, to look at what is said about Latino representation facilitates a better understanding of the political context in which decisions about textbook adoption are made.

Having provided testimony on several occasions, I have observed recurrent themes and issues as well as specific types of critiques that are repeated regarding the textbooks up for adoption. These issues and critiques are expressed in both the oral as well as the written testimony and provide valuable insights into the kinds of issues that emerge regarding the representation of Latinos in U.S. history textbooks.

Hearings were held in the capital, Austin, on three dates in 2002: July 17, August 23, and September 11. A week prior to each hearing date was the deadline for receipt of written comments, thus the written comments for July 17 were submitted on July 10.

I decided to review the transcripts from one of the three public hearings regarding the U.S. history textbooks up for adoption. The importance of these hearings is underlined by the fact that if adopted, the selected texts will be used beginning Fall 2003, and continue in use for at least ten years into the future.

I selected the oral and written testimony for those two July dates for our review and analysis, mainly because both contained a considerable amount of testimony regarding Latino, Hispanic, or Mexican American issues. As with other testimonies, they also contained a wide variety of perspectives from university professors and students as well as from speakers with established educational and ideological organizations.

The oral hearings were held in Austin and were conducted in a public forum with the State Board of Education (SBOE) members as formal recipients of the testimony. As such, board members were free to ask questions and they did so quite often, making comments as well, in response to the testimony brought forward. This gave speakers additional time beyond the allotted three-minute maximum to further clarify and extend their arguments.

METHODS USED TO ANALYZE TESTIMONY

Like the TEKS and the textbook analyses above, this was also primarily a content analysis study. However, due to the nature of the data, namely oral and written testimony, the major investigative task consisted of identifying topics or themes related to the representation of Latinos in those U.S. history textbooks being considered for official adoption by the state of Texas.

In order to gain a deeper understanding of the textbook adoption process during this cycle, I also engaged in the process as a participant observer and presented testimony based on my analysis of two textbooks and the TEKS. This aspect of the study will be more fully discussed later below.

For the purposes of the content analysis of spoken testimony, I identified one date, July 17, 2002, and reviewed the oral presentations for that day. This consisted of noting specifically everyone who presented any remarks related to the Hispanic, Latino, Mexican, or Mexican American experience, and also identifying the specific topic or theme they addressed.

In addition to the speaker and the topic, I also noted for each Latino related item, whether the particular issue had to do with either of three types of critiques or a combination thereof. From previous experience as a participant observer and from having reviewed other testimony, I noticed that there are at least three basic types of critiques made in these hearings, can conveniently be labeled the "ABCs" of textbook criticism. The three types of critiques are:

Accuracy: The content is incorrect as a simple matter of fact in terms of dates, names, the actual occurrence of events, or other knowledge.

Bias: The content expresses a partisan, political, ethnocentric, religious or ideological perspective, usually to the exclusion of other views.

Content: There is significant content missing that could or does result in bias, inaccuracy, and/or misrepresentation of historical facts.

These served as useful criteria for categorizing the many types of critiques presented, with the clear understanding that some testimony may include two or all three of these. Keeping these three types of critiques in mind, I reviewed both the oral and written testimony related to Latino/Hispanic concerns, and determined how many of each type were presented.

In order to facilitate in the task of identifying speakers, themes, and types of critiques, I developed a "Checklist of Critiques by Type, Theme and Speaker" and utilized a separate one for the oral and written testimonies presented in July 2002. Please refer to Appendix H: Checklist of Critiques to view this instrument.

Under the "Who" column, not only was the speaker's name and affiliation noted, but I also used key letters to indicate whether the speaker was a P=professor, S=student, T=teacher, R=representing an organization, or C=private citizen, not openly affiliated with any group or organization.

In terms of accessing documents for the content analysis of public testimony, the Texas Education Agency made available through its web site a full transcript of the oral testimony presented on all three days in which they occurred. I was also able to obtain a copy of the written testimony associated with the July 17 hearing by sending a written request for this printed material. These were the two main documents used in this study, and the results of the content analyses from both were collected, tallied, compared and discussed.

PARTICIPANT OBSERVATION

As mentioned above, in addition to the content analyses of both oral and written testimony, I also took the opportunity of providing testimony on September 11, 2002, and submitted copies of my full testimony to the members of the State Board of Education (SBOE). The testimony was mostly based on a contrast and comparison study I had conducted regarding the quantity and quality of Latino content in two of the U. S. history textbooks up for adoption.

My testimony regarding these textbooks used specific examples from both texts to illustrate my findings that one textbook was superior to the other in its representation of Latino history and heritage. I also indicated in my testimony some of the key features that distinguish adequate from inadequate textbook coverage of Latinos. I had preceded my comments on the two textbooks with several critical statements about the absence of Latinos, Hispanic, Mexican, or any such term, in the entire TEKS for U.S. history.

Given the relevance of my research findings to the representation of Latinos in history textbooks, I presented this testimony with the deliberate intent of having this become part of the official public record of Texas. My presentation of these findings at that time was also motivated by the fact that it had been almost a decade since there had been public hearings on U.S. history textbooks and that it would be at least seven years before another opportunity would come again.

Being a participant in the process, and being involved in testimony provided insight not only into the process, but also into the personalities, organizations, themes, issues and agendas being explicitly or implicitly expressed on that day. This approach generated much valuable information not readily evident from even a detailed review of the oral and written testimony.

I also had the opportunity of meeting other Latinos engaged with in process, including professors, university students, and private citizens, who presented varied types of critiques. One presenter, Dr. Manuel Medrano, Professor of History at the University of Texas at Brownsville, was accompanied by several of his students, who also provided testimony. He even brought a special guest, Medal of Honor recipient, Sgt. José M. Lopez, in an attempt to dramatize his arguments in favor of Latino historical inclusion. According to Dr. Medrano, Sgt. Lopez now appears in several of those textbooks.

Many of us Latinos present that day sat together during lunch and took time to familiarize each other with our work in this and related areas, and to discuss strategies for networking and continued advocacy in textbook adoption.

Thus, the experience of providing testimony and engaging in participant observation provided the invaluable opportunity of better understanding the textbook adoption process by observing it from the inside. It also afforded me the privilege of contributing in some way to the effort of effecting changes in textbooks adoption policy by connecting with colleagues and joining my voice to theirs in speaking directly to the primary source of decision making power in Texas education, the State Board of Education.

DATA FROM 2002 TEXTBOOK TESTIMONY

As mentioned above, there were at least three basic types of critiques made, which can conveniently be labeled the "ABCs" of textbook criticism, namely: Accuracy, Bias and Content.

Keeping these three types of critiques in mind, I reviewed both the oral and written testimony related to Latino/Hispanic concerns, and determined how many of each type were presented. In addition to this typology of critiques, I also noted the themes or issues that were expressed in the testimony and who presented them.

Oral Testimony: July 17, 2002

On July 17, 2002 there were a total of sixty-seven speakers signed up to testify regarding social studies textbooks, however, due to a variety of circumstances forty-two were actually present to testify. Each speaker was allotted only three minutes for his/her oral presentation, although his/her time could be effectively extended by questions or comments from the State Board of Education before whom they spoke (TEA, 2002a).

Of those forty-two only fifteen speakers addressed issues directly related to Latinos, Hispanics, or Mexican Americans or to the history of Mexico or Latin America. Thirteen of those fifteen who addressed Latino related issues had Spanish surnames and were presumably of Hispanic descent themselves.

Using four general categories to identify these fifteen speakers according to how they self-identified: six were college students, four were college professors, three were representatives of organizations, and two spoke as private citizens. Thus, ten of the fifteen, or two-thirds of those who spoke on Latino issues, were from colleges or universities in Texas, and all of them were Latinos.

Although Latinos have only occasionally been involved before in the textbook adoption process in Texas, it seems that on this day there was significant Latino presence and involvement. It's also important to note that Mexican American college professors and their students were spearheading that engagement.

Given the nature of the testimony, it is possible to quantify the number of discrete critiques speakers made regarding textbooks. The fifteen who testified on Latino related issues, for example, made approximately thirty-nine specific critiques. As stated and defined above, these critiques can be categorized into three types, with A=Accuracy, B=Bias, and C=Content.

Sometimes a particular critique could involve two or more critiques, for example, both accuracy and bias, (AB) or any combination of two or three types (i.e. AC, BC, or ABC). Using this typology, the thirty-nine critiques were categorized and yielded the following results presented as a simple formula: *29C + 4BC + 3AC + 1AB + 1B + 1ABC = 39 Critiques*

It is important to note that by far the largest number of critiques (29C), were about content alone, more specifically about content that was missing from the textbook. Another eight critiques involved missing content, four of which also included issues of bias (4BC), three included problems with accuracy (3AC), and one involved all three types of critiques (1ABC).

Thus overall, thirty-seven of the thirty-nine Latino-related critiques had to do almost totally, or in part, with issues of missing content. Clearly, what is *not* said about Hispanics or Latinos, and more specifically about Mexicans or Mexican Americans, was by far the largest single type of criticism presented during this day of public hearings when it comes to Latino issues.

A variety of issues were presented by these fifteen speakers, and with a few exceptions, most of the issues had to do with U.S. history or Texas history textbooks. These thirty-nine critiques are listed in the below, beginning with those presented by students first, followed by those from professors, private citizens, and then organizational representatives.

College or University Students

1. Too little coverage of Aztec and Maya Civilizations
2. No mention of Hispanics fighting in World War II
3. Too little coverage of Cesar Chavez
4. No mention of the Delano Grape Strike
5. Too little on pre-Columbian civilizations and Columbian Exchange
6. Not enough on early Spanish settlements in Southwest
7. Not enough on Hispanic civil rights struggle
8. Mexican and Latin American revolutions not mentioned
9. Spanish conquest of Aztecs incomplete and biased
10. Violent conflicts between Anglos & Tejanos not mentioned
11. Pancho Villa, Francisco Madero, and Emma Tenayuca are missing
12. No mention of Hispanics in the Civil War
13. Mexican soldiers cast as evil murderers in Alamo (Bias)
14. No mention of obstacles to Latino voting rights
15. Of 640 pages in textbook, only 40 on women and minorities

Professors

1. Details missing on Olmec, Maya and Aztec civilizations
2. Not enough on Hispanic settlers, ranchos in New Spain & work ethic
3. Details missing on first battle of U.S. Mexican War
4. Name of Mexican soldiers in last U.S./Mexico War battle: Niños Heroes
5. Story of Mexican Americans not included adequately in textbooks
6. Mexican Rancheros helped American Revolutionary effort
7. One of the first long cattle drives in history not included
8. Mexican settlers were already in Texas before Anglos/missing info
9. Spanish-surnamed Tejanos were the only native defenders in Alamo
10. Texas as state, did not exist in 1826 as implied by textbook
11. Mexican Americans marginalized also in textbooks
12. Mexican American students stifled by textbook exclusion
13. Little coverage of Mexico, Latin America, and Hispanic influences
14. Puerto Rico not in U.S. map, labeled as "dependency" but not defined and status unclear

Private Citizens

1. Inadequate representation of Hispanics in textbooks
2. No section on Hispanic civil rights movement
3. No mention of litigation required to ensure Hispanic civil rights
4. Four outstanding Mexican Americans (Gus Garcia, Carlos Cadena, Dr. Hector Perez-Garcia, José Angel Gutierrez) missing from textbooks
5. Both Hispanic and non-Hispanics ignorant about Hispanic heroes
6. Spanish names of Alamo defenders not mentioned
7. Juan Seguin's contributions to Texas Revolution missing

Organizational Representatives

1. Border claims by Texans before Texas Revolution not accurate
2. U.S. payments to Mexico after Mexican American War, incorrect
3. Mexican American heroes missing from textbooks

As stated above and confirmed by this list, the vast majority of the issues or errors presented on this day of testimony were related to what is missing from textbooks related to the Latino experience. In terms of specific topics, some issues were raised concerning improper or insufficient attention paid to pre-Columbian civilizations of Ancient Mexico, namely Aztecs, Mayas, and Olmecs. However, the majority of critiques addressed the absence of Latinos in the context of U.S. and Texas history.

Especially emphasized was the fact that Hispanics were not being mentioned as contributing combatants in our most significant armed conflicts, especially the Civil War, the Texas Revolutionary War, and World War II. Also mentioned frequently, as missing or minimally covered, was information on the Mexican American civil rights movement.

Finally, although not reflected in the summarized list above, on at least four occasions, Latino college students made clear contrasts between the way Latinos were covered as opposed to the way African Americans were covered. One had to do with the Civil War, but three specifically mentioned how the African American civil rights movement got adequate coverage while that of Mexican Americans did not, or was completely excluded in the text.

Written Testimony: July 10, 2003

A close review of the materials submitted by July 10, 2003, revealed that for the most part, they are directly related to and supportive of the speakers' presentations on July 17. Thirty-five individuals submitted written documents in support of their statements; eight were students, four were professors, ten were private citizens, and thirteen were organizational representatives.

Almost half of these individuals, precisely seventeen, submitted critiques and comments that wholly or in part addressed issues related to Hispanics, Mexican Americans, Mexico or Latin America. All but four of those seventeen had Spanish surnames.

Most of the Latino-related issues expressed in writing were identical to those presented orally. However, other issues did emerge from the written documents that for reasons of time and emphasis were not articulated. Moreover, those issues mentioned in both spoken hearings and in written comments usually received much more detailed treatment in written form, as expected.

Below are the eighteen Latino-related issues contained in the written comments, but not mentioned in the oral testimony.

College or University Students

1. Pancho Villa portrayed as only a villain in both Mexico and U.S.
2. No mention of Cuban and Central American immigration to U.S.

Professors

1. Only two Hispanics in hundreds of biographies of key Americans
2. Geographic location and discussion of Mexico is confusing
3. Terms "Latino" "Hispanic" "Mexican American" used without clear explanation of each
4. Both "push" and "pull" factors of Latino immigration ignored
5. Sandinistas, democratically elected, but labeled as "dictators"
6. No information on current embargo against Cuba
7. No mention of Central American immigration
8. No mention of "Reagan Wars" in Central America and U.S. support of death squads
9. No mention of the fact that the Treaty of Guadalupe Hidalgo also included provisions to respect Spanish and Mexican land grants, but that Congress voted against it

Private Citizen

1. Not enough photos of women and minorities
2. Too many photos of White males

Organizational Representatives

1. The nature of Anglo vs. Spanish early settlements not contrasted clearly enough
2. "Deaf" Smith got more profile in text than did Zavala and others during the Texas Revolution
3. There was no mention of leaders, such as Cortez, and Father Hidalgo in "colonial" Texas
4. Spain's contribution to American Revolution was profound, but not mentioned in any textbook
5. Spanish General Galvez played a key role in defeating British forces in southern Gulf coast during Revolutionary War; however, this is not mentioned

When considering this list of eighteen critiques from the written comments together with the thirty-nine from those generated in the oral testimony, it is abundantly clear that the fifty-seven critiques are overwhelmingly concerned with issues of exclusion or missing content rather than factual accuracy or intentional bias.

It is significant to note that in both oral and written testimony, especially when it comes to Latino exclusion, presenters emphasized or at least implied that this missing information does affect the overall bias or perspective of the historical narrative and could, in come cases, even effectively present inaccurate portrayals or interpretations.

Nevertheless, this focus on what is not in the textbook also reflects the reality that despite occasional incorrect factoids or obvious bias, when it comes to Latinos in history textbooks, the issue is more of underrepresentation than misrepresentation.

Participant Observation: Textbook Public Hearings

On September 11, 2002, I had a third opportunity to testify before the State Board of Education (SBOE) in Austin regarding textbooks. In 1991 I had presented a textbook critique with the mentorship of Dr. Linda Salvucci, an historian then at Trinity University. A year later, the 1992 hearings took place, and provided Texas with the social studies textbooks used until quite recently, Spring 2003.

For that key hearing I helped organize and served as the coordinator for an ad-hoc committee, the *Multicultural Alliance of San Antonio* (MASA), which brought together academic historians, teachers, college students, and even high school students to review textbooks and testify regarding the representation of Latinos and women in literature and social studies texts (Texas Education Agency, 1992).

Thus, by the time I was making preparations for my testimony for September, 2002 I had become quite familiar with the process, and was also becoming more aware of the subtle nuances involved in presenting an effective testimony. I also obtained a more accurate view of how sophisticated and well funded were the reviews and testimony of certain politically conservative organizations that had for decades been criticizing textbooks in Texas.

Among those observations I made are that the process for providing testimony, though not inherently difficult, does require initiative, persistence, and attention to detail to be done effectively. For this reason alone, organizations and groups such as those organized by college professors and their students, offer a distinct advantage over any individual's effort to testify.

Providing a written document one week before the testimony is, of course, advantageous permitting an extended opportunity to include much more detailed commentary and recommendations far beyond what three minutes of speaking orally would permit. I also noticed that providing a short, three to four page summary of main points to the SBOE at the time of testimony, also ensures that these points are not missed. It also creates options of presenting tables, charts, maps, or other visually effective evidence to bolster one's arguments. Thus providing written and visual documentation is a strategic and necessary part of any truly effective testimony, as we learned from our efforts with MASA, especially when circumstances could prevent scholars, students or private citizens from actually attending the hearings in person.

Among those organizations that had been providing testimony on textbooks for decades, many already had a statewide or national reputation. Among those I have heard, and sometimes encountered, are the well-known Mel and Norma Gabler's Educational Research Analysts, perhaps the godparents of right-wing textbook critics. During the 2002 hearings, other influential conservative organizations, participating with numerous individual presenters and extensive written documentation, included the following:

• Texas Public Policy Foundation
• Texas Citizens for a Sound Economy
• Texas Society—Daughters of the American Revolution
• The Eagle Forum—Austin

It is interesting to note that the Texas Public Policy Foundation (TPPF), according to the testimony of its members, had enough resources to commission sixteen reviewers, including academics and other professionals in their fields, who generated a 98-page report. The TPPF spent nearly $100,000 in this particular review, a through one that discovered and documented 533 textbook "errors" (TEA, 2002).

There were also educational organizations providing testimony, namely the Texas Council for the Social Studies, as well as a few politically progressive organizations, including Americans United for Separation of Church and State, and the Texas Freedom Network (TFN). As a watchdog and policy institute opposed to religious right wing influence, the TFN has become thoroughly involved in the Texas textbook adoption process and is a reliable source for related information.

There were also specific Latino professors who either provided individual testimony (Dr. José Limón of UT Austin), or did so in conjunction with their students (Dr. Manuel Medrano of UT Brownsville). Other Latino professors testifying included Dr. Rolando Hinojosa and Dr. Emilio Zamora, both of UT Austin, as well as Dr. José Angel Gutierrez of UT Arlington, and an historic figure himself as a civil rights activist and founder of La Raza Unida Party.

Outside of a few Latino academics and their students, however, the only Latino organization that was represented in testimony for the 2002 cycle was the National Council of La Raza, and even that was more of an individual than an organizational effort.

It cannot be emphasized enough that certain organizations, especially the more conservative ones such as TPPF and Texas Citizens for a Sound Economy, regularly receive much more media access and attention and were advantaged not only with more resources but with more testimony time courtesy of some SBOE members who asked friendly questions and/or made supportive comments.

The many advantages and the considerable influence religious and politically conservative organizations have at these textbook hearings were clearly evident to me and others who have observed for years.

What made the 2002 hearings different, however, was that perhaps for the first time, Latino presenters, including myself, were asked friendly questions and were supplemented with supportive statements, not surprisingly, mostly from the Latino SBOE members.

The hearings transcripts document, for example, that one board member, Ms. Mary Helen Berlanga, was impressed enough with my presentation that she requested that I conduct a similar review of all the other U.S. history textbooks, in addition to the two I had already done. She, and to a lesser extent, Dr. Allen, also asked several questions and made comments in response to which I was free to expand on my statements considerably (TEA, 2002b). This same opportunity was also provided by both Latino and non-Latino SBOE members to other Latino presenters, especially the professors, thus permitting all of us to further extend our comments, not only about the textbooks *per se*, but also about the TEKS and the textbook adoption process itself.

Participating in the September 11 hearing, precisely one year from that now historic date, gave me the opportunity to make more profound comments about the meaning of patriotism and democracy in the context of a truly authentic and multicultural telling of our history. An honest statement of my beliefs, including the motivations that drove my research, is quoted below as relevant data:

> Love of our nation goes beyond grieving its tragedies and celebrating its victories. It includes adherence to the belief in our highest democratic principles. These very principles compel many of us to be here today, to insure that when the story of America is told and studied in public schools, all the people who helped make our nation great will be included. But much too often, this has not been the case; in study after study I reviewed for my doctoral thesis, the exclusion, or misrepresentation of racial and ethnic

minorities, and especially Latinos, is well documented. The proper inclusion of Latinos in the U.S. history curriculum and textbooks is not driven nor justified by acquiescence to pressure groups or political correctness— on the contrary, it is founded on the democratic principle that the story of America cannot be told completely, nor accurately, if Latinos or other minorities are misrepresented or left out (TEA, 2002 b).

Among the many opportunities for learning that I gained from participating and observing the textbook adoption process, is that of personally meeting and informally consulting with Dr. Manuel Medrano, his students and other Latino professors who were there, most of whom testified. I not only listened closely to their testimony, but also talked over lunch with them about what can be done collectively and collaboratively in the future.

It was obvious to me, for example, that although there was much criticism by my Latino colleagues of most textbooks' poor treatment of the Mexican American civil rights movement, nobody had reviewed the high school level Holt text, and thus discovered, as I did, that they had an excellent and truly outstanding section on this very topic.

The problem is that we were not coordinating our efforts so as to avoid duplication and to ensure maximum coverage of all social studies textbooks.

Recognizing that we do not have many thousands of dollars to spend on textbook reviews, as does, the TPPF, we concluded that establishing an informal network would at least keep us in communication with each other. Already some academics were attempting to establish such an organization, and the general feeling among most of us was that we had achieved something significant and that we could only do better in the future.

Latinos in Adoption Process: A Summary

To conclude this chapter, I will briefly summarize the major findings that emerged from the testimony and other data regarding the presence of Latinos in this most recent textbook adoption process in 2002.

    a.   Latinos did have a recognizable and significant presence in both the oral and written testimony of July 2002.

    b.   Many Latino-related issues and concerns were expressed in both forms of testimony.

    c.   Most critiques about Latino representation focused more on what was missing, rather than what was wrong in textbooks.

d. There was a wide range of Latino related testimony in terms of length and complexity.

e. Several presenters spoke about the negative effects for both Latino and non-Latino students of having Latinos under- represented in social studies textbooks.

Given the trends that I have observed over the last decade in textbook adoption, it is logical to predict that in the future, Latinos as an advocacy group will continue to have increasing and consistent presence in the textbook adoption process of Texas. Religious right and conservative groups will probably continue to wield their usual influence, but it will be increasingly challenged by such organizations as the Texas Freedom Network or others unwilling to yield without a fight in this important battlefield of our never ending Culture Wars.

Chapter Seven
Summary, Interpretations, and Recommendations

BRIEF SUMMARY OF FINDINGS FROM ENTIRE STUDY

As a mixed method investigation, the findings from this effort are derived from a variety of studies and sources, yet the underlying objective for each component was the same: to identify, document, and analyze the presence of Latinos in the teaching of U.S. history in Texas. Use of this mixed method was based on the sound and verifiable assumption that many factors impinge on what is taught and how in the classroom, including the TEKS curriculum standards, the adopted textbooks, and the standardized tests.

In addition to these structural factors, there are the classroom teachers' own perspectives, preferences and preparation that ultimately determine methods and content. Finally, there is the role of public testimony that interjects elements of political and religious ideology into the very process of textbook adoption.

As fully described in the above chapters, I decided to conduct separate but related studies in four general areas:

1. TEKS statewide curriculum standards
2. Textbooks officially adopted by the state
3. Teachers' perspectives and preferences
4. Testimony presented in the most recent (2002) textbook hearings

The major and most significant findings from each of these areas of study are briefly summarized below.

1. Texas Essential Knowledge and Skills (TEKS)

The findings presented below for this area emerged from a thorough investigation I conducted on the content of the TEKS for U.S. history at both the high school and middle school to determine the presence of Latino (or Hispanic) individuals, groups, events, experience, and concepts, or the mention of any generic category into which Latinos could be classified, such as "immigrant" or "ethnic minority."

The same search of both TEKS standards were done for African Americans and American Indians, and the findings were classified, tallied, discussed, and displayed on three tables. Table 1 displays the findings from the first part of U.S. history TEKS, Table 2 contains findings for the second part, and Table 3 combines data from both tables. Please refer to Appendix A: Four Levels of TEKS to view the three tables.

Among the most significant findings was that

(A) In all the TEKS for U.S. history not once is any Latino individual mentioned by name, and neither is any individual American Indian, whereas four African American individuals are thus mentioned.

(B) Nowhere is the term Latino, Hispanic, Mexican, Mexican American, Chicano, Puerto Rican, Cuban, or any other group name for Latinos ever mentioned. Only once in these TEKS is any term for African American or American Indian used.

(C) There were ten events or concepts mentioned which had some direct relation to or clear association with African Americans. For Latinos there were six, and for American Indians, there were two.

(D) In terms of categories mentioned in the TEKS into which any of the three groups could be classified, Latinos had ten, African American had eight and American Indians, had seven.

It should be noted that although Latinos had ten items in general finding (D), since this refers to generic terms such as "immigrant" and "ethnic minority," it does not guarantee that U.S. history teachers will necessarily include Latinos, and if so, it does not specify the extent to which, nor how, Latinos will be brought into the narrative. What this means is that, based on the TEKS, the possibility does exist for some Latino coverage, but their inclusion in the classroom narrative depends on how well Latino immigrants, or Latinos as significant minorities, are covered in the textbooks. Of course, it also depends on the preferences or preparation of the teacher.

Even the events which are Latino-related in finding (C), such as the Mexican American War, or the Spanish American War, do not compel the teacher to bring into discussion the perspective or historical experiences of Puerto Ricans or Cubans during the latter conflict or of Mexicans or Mexican Americans in the former. Thus, again, only the possibility of Latino coverage exists, and whether it happens or not depends on the textbook content and the teachers' practice, as well as the other structural factors mentioned above.

Perhaps the most surprising or significant findings are (A) and (B). It is quite astounding that even in Texas not one Latino individual is mentioned by name in the entire TEKS for U.S. history at both levels, whereas four African Americans were thus named. It is also surprising that with the multitude of terms used for Latino groups here in the United States, not one is present in these entire curriculum standards.

Thus the following three realities emerged from this study: 1) these curriculum guidelines were established in the most Latino-influenced state in the nation; 2) there is an officially sanctioned discussion of civil rights, immigrants, and ethnic minorities in the Texas TEKS for U.S. history; and 3) despite these two realities, no Latino individuals, groups or movements were deemed worthy of specific mention in either of the two year-long course standards. This raises serious questions, among them, the reasonable suspicion that the exclusion of Latinos was deliberate and not merely circumstantial.

Yet, to assume deliberate intent is only conjecture. What isn't in question is that the exclusion of Latinos from the U.S. history curriculum standards for Texas, astounding as it may seem, is a demonstrated and undeniable fact.

2. State Adopted U.S. History Textbooks

There were two separate studies of U.S. history textbooks, each one involving content analyses and comparisons among the texts. The first study involved three textbooks and was more thorough in its identification, classification, and analyses of both textual and visual content related to the Latino experience. The second study involved two textbooks and provided a more general overview of Latino-related content in both for the purposes of contrast and comparison.

For the first study, three of the six high school U.S. history textbooks officially adopted by TEA and used for the last ten years until Spring 2003, were reviewed:

Berkin, Carol, et al. (1992). *American voices: A history of the United States, Volume II: 1865 to the present.* Glenview, IL: Scott Foresman.

Davidson, J.W., Lytle, M.H. and Stoff, M.B. (1992). *American journey: The quest for liberty since 1865.* Englewood Cliffs, NJ:
Prentice Hall.

Garraty, John. (1992). *The story of America, Vol. 2: 1865 to the
present.* Austin, TX: Holt, Rinehart and Winston.

As described in detail above in Chapter 4, each textbook was reviewed,
beginning with the index and table of contents, and every sentence related
to the Latino experience was counted and categorized by topic and by
national origin.

The information on each text was then summarized on a table. In
terms of the overall quantity, as determined by the number of sentences
dealing with the Latino experience, that number ranged from a total of 376
sentences in the Prentice Hall textbook to 180 in the Scott Foreman text.
The Holt text had 265 sentences. (Please refer to Appendix B: Textbook
Tables for a view of all three tables.)

As expected, the vast majority of these sentences in all three texts
related to Mexican Americans. In fact, in all textbooks, there was the same
pattern of coverage as measured by the number of sentences, with Mexican
Americans having the most, followed by Latinos in general, then Puerto
Ricans, and finally Cubans with the least number. In a sense, this almost
reflects the population demographics of each group since Cubans are the
smallest of the three most populous Latino national origin groups, and
Mexican Americans are by far the largest.

Of the seven general topical areas within that Latino coverage, the
three that received the most attention in these textbooks were (a) Characteristics and Experiences, (b) Problems and Accomplishments, and (c)
Leaders. The topics with least coverage, and this was consistent in all three
texts, were the reasons why Latinos immigrated to the United States, when
this occurred, and where they resided in the nation.

In terms of quantity as a whole, it is also important to note what percentage of the entire textbook narrative is dedicated to Latinos. Using as an
example the Holt textbook with an intermediate number of Latino-related
sentences, its 265 sentences would yield just fewer than 18 full pages of full
text. Given that the Holt book is just over 630 pages long, it means that a
mere 3% of the book has text focusing on the Latino experience.

Without doing all the calculations for the other two textbooks which
have approximately the same total number of pages, it is evident that a few
more or fewer percentage points do not alter the overall obvious conclusion

that given their population and historical significance to this nation, Latinos are still quite underrepresented in these U.S. history textbooks

To assess the qualitative aspect of these three textbooks, the following five criteria mentioned in Chapter 4 were used.

1. Factual accuracy
2. Inclusion of key leaders, dates, events, issues, contributions
3. Presentation of Latino views or perspectives
4. Agency attributed to Latino leaders, organizations, or people
5. Connections made between past and present

There was considerable variety in the qualitative aspects of these three textbooks. Thus, it was quite difficult to make clear comparisons among them in terms of quality. What proved helpful was to document the extent to which the passages in each text met the five qualitative criteria. When comparing the quality of the longer passages related to Latinos in these texts, for example, it becomes evident that most of these passages in the Prentice Hall textbook meet four or more of the five qualitative criteria.

Averaging out the ratings (on a scale from 1 to 5) for all six major Latino-related sections in the Prentice Hall text would yield a 3.67 rating. Doing the same with the sections in the Holt text generated a rating of 3.25, and for the Scott Foresman text, that rating would be a 2.7.

Yet, these numbers only reveal part of the qualitative aspect. The Scott Foresman textbook authors, for example, had the courage to deal honestly with certain issues such as discrimination, forced deportations, and political empowerment often better than the other two texts.

Because of the mixed characteristics in each text, it is difficult to clearly declare any of the three texts superior in every way in terms of quality of Latino coverage. Consequently, the above criteria based ratings must be considered in conjunction with other factors, including the kinds of topics textbook authors are willing to address and how objectively and accurately they do so.

Nevertheless, it is very important to note that a clear pattern emerges when considering quantity and quality together. The text with the most pages related to Latinos, the Prentice Hall, also has the highest quality rating; conversely, the text with the lowest quality rating, the ScottForesman, also had the smallest number of Latino-related pages. Thus, all three texts fall into the same qualitative-quantitative continuum as displayed below:

	Qualitative Rating	Quantity of Pages
Prentice Hall	3.67	376
Holt, R&W	3.25	265
ScottForesman	2.7	180

It is also significant to note the irony that among these three textbooks, the one with the lowest quality and quantity rating, namely Scott Foresman, happens to be the textbook officially adopted by Northside I.S.D., the largest district in predominantly Hispanic San Antonio, and a district with over 50% Latino students.

The second U.S. history textbook study involved a contrast comparison of two textbooks in terms of both quantity and quality of information related to Latinos. Both of these high school level U.S. history textbooks, adopted by the state for use during the next ten years, were targeted for review:

> Boyer, Paul & Stuckey, Sterling. (2003). *The American nation*. Austin, TX: Holt, Rinehart and Winston.
> Cayton, Perry, Reed & Winkler. (2003). *America: Pathways to the present*. Englewood Cliffs, NJ: Prentice Hall.

The most striking contrast between these is the sheer difference in the scope and depth of coverage. The Holt textbook deals with a wide variety of topics related to Mexican Americans, some consisting of a few paragraphs, while others taking several pages with more detailed and thorough descriptions. By contrast, the Prentice Hall text covers fewer topics related to Latinos, particularly Mexican Americans, and does not enrich its presentation with as many quotes, graphics, and primary sources as does Holt

Overall, the quality of writing related to Latinos is superior in the Holt text; topics are better elaborated and concepts are explained more fully as well. It is clear that one publisher has invested more effort, space and resources to presenting the Latino story than the other.

Considering the major findings from both textbook studies, we can make some general statements. There has been much improvement in the representation of Latinos in textbooks over the last two decades. Yet, no U.S. history textbook reviewed presents the full range of Latino diversity, in terms of national origin, racial mixture, cultural heritage, social class, and levels of assimilation. Moreover, the many Latino contributions in the areas of military service, cattle ranching, civil rights, education, law, literature, music and the arts have not been adequately documented in any single textbook.

3. Teachers' Perspectives and Preferences

As fully described above in Chapter 5, this was a three-part study consisting of individual interviews with twelve U.S. history teachers, a focus group of four teachers, and sixteen course content checklists.

The individual interviews generated a wealth of data that was extracted and analyzed. From the wide variety of findings discussed above, we can discuss several implications and draw some definite conclusions.

First of all, considering the structural conditions over which teachers have little or no control, most participants were critical of the TAAS standardized statewide test, yet generally satisfied with the TEKS standards upon which the TAAS is supposedly based. They had some critiques of the textbooks as well. This implies that U.S. history teachers do not resist standards *per se*, but are critical of how these are assessed with the use of a standardized test.

The issue of time, that is, the lack of sufficient time to cover the required content, let alone that which teachers prefer, was consistently repeated as a major problem closely related to the difficulty in including women and minorities, let alone doing this adequately.

Although responses were not related to the grade level U.S. history teachers taught, gender did play a role in the content participants most preferred to teach. Females were least interested in battles and wars, while males tended to have more interest in these conflicts. Perhaps this reflects the socialization of males towards violence in our culture, whereby they feel more comfortable discussing the details of battles and bloody struggles than most females do.

The length of experience did also seem to correlate with participants' views on such structural aspects as the TEKS, TAAS and the textbooks. Those with less experience tended to have significantly more criticisms of these official curriculum constraints than did their more experienced veterans. This could mean that younger teachers have been trained to value more flexible, experiential, cooperative, and student-centered approaches to instruction than the older teachers.

The ethnoracial identity of participants did have some correlation with their responses; there was a greater tendency for the four minority participants to make references to the exclusion of women and people of color from the official curriculum. This is not surprising.

Several unsolicited references or statements regarding minorities or issues of diversity were made during the interviews.

- On four occasions, four participants mentioned "women" in the content of the curriculum, two were male, and two were female.

- Only three participants mentioned either women or minorities when discussing those eras, events, or individuals of special interest to them.
- On eight occasions, five participants mentioned "Hispanics" and the need to include them in the curriculum.

Although most participants did make statements about the exclusion of minorities at some point during their interviews, and obviously attached some importance to teaching multiculturally, their responses to the course content checklist revealed that in actual practice, minorities, like women, are consistently left out, as will be discussed below.

In terms of the focus group, perhaps the single most significant finding is that in the entire hour and a half session, despite ample opportunities to do so, especially since women and minorities were discussed and some ethnoracial groups were even mentioned by name, not once was the term Latino, Hispanic, Mexican American, or any other similar name ever mentioned by participants.

Other findings confirmed that such structural conditions as the TEKS, standardized tests, textbooks and the lack of time were very influential in determining teachers' content choices.

As in the individual interviews, the TEKS elicited a variety of views, including the lack of coverage on women and minorities. Most participants viewed the textbooks as inadequate and outdated. Of all structural conditions, the standardized tests were the most thoroughly criticized for their distortion of the curriculum, their negative effects on time and scheduling, and the restrictions they placed on the teaching of history itself.

Lack of time and student characteristics, such as lack of proper skills or sufficient interest, were also cited as obstacles to using the innovative instruction and teaching either the required or preferred content.

Overall, the responses from focus group participants and individual interviewees concurred on some very significant points. Most important among them for our investigation was that structural factors over which teachers have no control exerted a hindering influence on teachers' ability to include women, minorities, and Latinos in particular into the course narrative.

In terms of the course content, in checklists filled out by all sixteen participants, perhaps the most revealing finding is that of all the names of individuals and groups included in their history courses, Latinos are overwhelmingly the most excluded from the course curriculum.

4. Textbook Testimony

With this study of testimony presented on the U.S. history textbooks being considered for adoption, I intended to document the type of Latino-related issues being discussed and to ascertain the level of Latino participation in these influential hearings.

For the review and analysis, I selected the oral and written testimony presented in July 2002 mainly because both contained a considerable amount of references regarding Latino, Hispanic, or Mexican American issues. As with other testimonies, these also contained a wide variety of perspectives from university professors and students as well as from speakers representing established educational and ideological organizations.

As described in Chapter 6, I conducted systematic content analyses of both the oral and written testimony that generated considerable data. I also engaged as a participant-observer during the September 11 public hearings in Austin to gain further insight on the process itself, directly observe the testimony and converse with other Latinos presenting testimony that day. The essential findings from these two efforts can be summarized thus:

a. Latinos did have a recognizable and significant presence in both the oral and written testimony of July and September 2002.
b. Many Latino-related issues and concerns were expressed in both oral and written testimony.
c. Most critiques about Latino representation focused more on what was missing, rather than on what was inaccurate in textbooks.
d. There was a wide range of Latino-related testimony in terms of length and complexity.
e. Several presenters spoke about the negative effects for both Latino and non-Latino students of having Latinos underrepresented in social studies textbooks.

Given the trends I have observed over the last decade in textbook adoption, it is logical to predict that in the future, Latinos as an advocacy group will continue to have increasing and consistent presence in the textbook adoption process of Texas.

INTERPRETATIONS FROM EXISTING THEORY

The findings from the data correspond in several ways with both multicultural education theory (MET) and critical race theory (CRT). Below is a review of the implications these theories have, whenever appropriate, to our findings on the TEKS, textbooks, textbook testimonies, and teachers perspectives' and preferences.

The findings on the Texas Essential Knowledge and Skills (TEKS) have a close relationship with Banks' four distinct approaches to public schools' attempts at teaching multiculturally. The TEKS does not encourage students to decide about social issues, let alone take actions to solve them. Nor does the TEKS structure the curriculum to enable students to view history from diverse ethnic or cultural perspectives. Thus, neither the Social Action nor the Transformation approaches are used.

Given the intent of the TEKS, there is no focus on heroes or holidays *per se*, at least not significant Latino heroes or holidays; thus, it does not use the Contributions Approach. If anything the TEKS seems to utilize an Additive Approach whereby multicultural content is "added to the curriculum without changing its structure." Even in this approach, however, when it comes to Latinos, specific content is absent or minimal in the TEKS, and Latino inclusion exists only as a possibility under some generic category such as "immigrant" or "ethnic minority."

In terms of CRT, the underrepresentation of ethnic minorities in the TEKS confirms the CRT concept that racism is a normal occurrence, and not an aberration, thus making it more difficult to address. It also confirms that the CRT concept of the "black-white binary" is operating since the African American civil rights movement is viewed as the only civil rights movement worthy of mention and study, and the fact that that all other struggles by ethnoracial minorities are somehow subsumed under that experience.

From the data gathered regarding textbooks, with the underrepresentation of minorities and especially Latinos, the CRT concept of racism being the normal state of affairs is confirmed. Although through the efforts of many activists in the textbook adoption process, there has been some considerable improvement, my findings, together with those of other researchers, confirm that changing textbooks regarding their more subtle racist elements is difficult work.

On the other hand, some textbooks have begun to reflect part of the CRT concept which holds that "each race or ethnic group has its own origins and ever evolving history," since there are separate sections in most of these texts which deal with the Latino experience. This also means that the "black-white binary" which affects the TEKS, does not exert a dominant influence over the way textbooks cover African Americans and other ethnoracial groups.

When considering textbooks in the light of multicultural education theory, specifically Banks' four approaches, it is clearly evident that overall U.S. history texts use both the Contributions and Additive Approach in their presentation of content related to racial and ethnic minorities, particularly Latinos. There is little or no content in textbooks that provides students with Latino perspectives, although the events covered do provide ample opportunity, let alone obligation, to do so. Neither is there any attempt in these texts to encourage students to make decisions or to take action on important issues; on the contrary students, are asked to memorize dates, names, and other factoids with little or no opportunity to evaluate options or differing perspectives. Thus, neither the Transformation nor Social Action approaches are evident in the U.S. history textbooks used for the last ten years or those to be used in the coming decade.

In terms of the textbook testimony, many speakers pointed out and decried the relative absence of Latino representation in textbooks, but some also mentioned the exclusion of any Latino perspectives from the textbook narrative. Whereas textbooks were incomplete in their application of Bank's Contributions and Additive approaches, according to speakers, textbooks did not make any attempts at utilizing the Transformation or Social Action approaches. Thus the testimony was, for the most part, in close agreement with the findings and interpretations of our own textbook analyses.

Several key statements also related well with some CRT concepts. Among them, speakers confirmed that the CRT concept which holds that each ethnoracial group has its own origins and ever-evolving history. Many spoke to that effect, and even made statements contrasting the Latino experience, especially the Mexican American civil rights movement, with that of African Americans. Another CRT concept holds that Latino and other ethnics, due to their distinct experiences, may communicate to their "White" counterparts, "certain matters that they (Whites) otherwise are unlikely to know." This was demonstrated on several occasions when Latino professors and students, including myself, pointed out historical events, facts, or perspectives which constituted new information for most Anglo board members present, who admitted not knowing about these before.

In considering the teachers' perspectives and preferences from both the individual interviews and the focus group, several MET and CRT concepts become quite evident. In terms of Banks' four approaches, teachers consistently criticized the textbooks for barely including women and minorities, and when textbooks did so, it was using the Contributions or Additive approaches. Essentially, it was the same critique made my many speakers in the textbook hearings; namely that there was no attempt to utilize the Transformation approach. That is, there was no inclusion in the textbooks of the perspectives of racial and ethnic minorities.

On several occasions, teachers did express recognition consistent with the CRT contention that "each race or ethnic group has its own origins and ever evolving history." There was also some indirect confirmation of the normalcy of racism in our society, and the difficulty in addressing it, a fundamental CRT premise. One opinion that emerged more clearly during the focus group session was that teacher training and courses in colleges and universities did not adequately prepare future teachers with the background information and skills to combat racism or ethnic prejudice.

Considering all the data from these component studies as a whole, there were tendencies identified by my analyses as well as by textbook testimonies and teachers' perspectives, that the teaching of U.S. history takes either an Assimilation or Amalgamation view of how minorities adapt to the U.S. lifestyle. According to Sleeter and Grant (1994), these two views assume that eventually the values and cultural traditions of minorities will be replaced by that of the dominant group or be incorporated into a larger social synthesis.

On very few occasions, and sometimes most notably in textbooks, were the Classical or Modified Cultural Pluralism views, whereby minority groups maintain their values and lifestyles, upheld.

LIMITATIONS

As with every investigation, there are some obvious limitations with this collection of studies. Whereas the TEKS study was quite complete in its coverage of both documents related to the teaching of U.S. history, not all the textbooks currently being used nor up for future adoption were reviewed and analyzed due to time limitations. Nevertheless, I am confident that the general findings about the underrepresentation of Latinos can be verified if the same approach to review and analyses were replicated with the other textbooks not reviewed. It is very unlikely that a complete review of all textbooks will generate data contradictory to the fundamental findings and conclusions derived from my review of selected texts.

In terms of the textbooks testimony, only one of the three days of oral testimony was reviewed, as was only one of three sets of written testimony. It's likely that other themes and topics were presented in addition to those revealed from my review.

Nevertheless, since my focus was specifically on issues related to Latino representation, I believe that the July testimonies were probably exemplary of the kinds of issues raised in regards to Latinos in August and September. As a participant observer in the September hearing, I perceived this was the case.

Perhaps the most obvious limitations of this entire investigation were evident in the three-part study of teachers' perspectives and preferences. Not because of the methodology per se, but because the numbers were not large enough, nor were the participants randomly selected so as to permit definite generalizations about the attitudes of U.S. history teachers in the Northside I.S.D., let alone the city or the state.

In the case of the focus group, I would have preferred at least two separate groups with more participants, including women, but logistics did not allow this to happen in the allotted time frame.

However, both the interviews and focus group studies did provide a sound foundation for the later development of a larger survey that could be more widely distributed and randomized within gender, ethnoracial, and experience categories to permit generalizations and comparisons. They also provide useful models for conducting additional interviews and focus groups on the same or similar topics. That sound foundation derives from the wealth of information we obtained from both these studies regarding the structural, personal, and social factors that influence teachers' content choices. With this knowledge we could design a much more targeted and meaningful survey and have more significant focus group discussions around identified issues and concerns that emerged from the responses of teacher's themselves.

Finally, in terms of the course content checklists, I believe that they have been pilot tested well with this investigation, and could perhaps with minor changes, be ready for much wider distribution that will permit a greater degree of generalization about teachers' content choices in the actual classroom. This is important because, regardless of what the TEKS or textbooks say, and despite the restricting influence of the standardized test, history teachers always exercise a measure of flexibility and choice when it comes to what is covered and how.

IMPLICATIONS

Taken together, the implications of this multifaceted investigation are clear. Despite the growing numbers and influence of Latinos, and regardless of the pivotal role they have played as individuals and as groups in our nation's history, they are still receiving little or no attention in the history classrooms of Texas, a state in which their presence has endured for centuries.

The reasons for this may be quite complex, and probably include the fact that many teachers, being products of our public education system, are themselves misinformed and perhaps even ignorant about Latino history and heritage. Some teachers in our study, honestly and openly admitted to having such limitations in their ability and inclination to cover Latino topics.

Another set of reasons, confirmed by this investigation, is that the standards established for the U.S. history curriculum (the TEKS), the vehicles used to teach it (the textbooks), and the instrument used to assess student learning, (the standardized test), all contribute in their own way to the exclusion of Latinos from the history classroom.

One of the most significant findings from this investigation is the powerful influence exerted by structural impediments to Latino curricular inclusion, and not only the TEKS, textbooks, and tests, but also teacher education and in-service training which do not prepare classroom teachers with the knowledge, skills and attitudes for effectively instructing in an inclusive, multicultural way.

Among the implications of this study are that Texas students from Kindergarten through 12th grade have at best an incomplete and spotty knowledge of Latino history, contributions and perspectives from their public schooling. Meanwhile, the mass media that impacts their thinking most powerfully, namely television and films, continues to exclude, marginalize or criminalize the image of Latinos in their minds.

What makes this more destructively ironic is that over a third of those K-12 Texas students are themselves Latinos, whose self-esteem, ethnic identity, and informed citizenship are eroded and damaged.

What this ultimately means is that there are entire generations of American students, now graduated and in leadership, influential or pivotal roles in our society, who have little or no knowledge of the history, culture, contributions, experience and perspectives of what is today the largest ethnic minority group in America. What this implies for race relations, social cohesion, and cross-cultural interaction is difficult to ascertain.

Obviously, Americans have other sources of information about Latinos than their formal schooling, and that is precisely the problem. When the mass media, and its most powerful vehicles, television and films, consistently present stereotypes, misinformation and distortions of who Latinos really are, then the burden falls on schools, colleges and universities to fulfill their responsibility of public education, and in the most basic sense, play their proper role in this regard.

What this investigation has shown is that in Texas, a most Latino-infused state, the system of public education has failed in its most fundamental duty of educating the public about a large group of people with whom Texans have lived, worked, and shared a wider community for over a century.

For college-educated Latinos, who have sought and obtained alternative and authentic sources of information on their history and heritage, this particular failure of public schooling is a frustrating obstacle. It is, nevertheless, one that can and has been overcome on an individual basis. But for millions of Latinos, who don't complete their formal education and who don't actively seek out alternative sources of information, there is a huge gap of ignorance about their own history, identity, and potentialities that affects not only their self-esteem, but also their entire worldview.

In short, all Americans, our entire civil society, and especially Latinos, are diminished and immeasurably harmed by this widespread ignorance about the largest, and one of the oldest, most significant ethnic groups in our nation.

RECOMMENDATIONS FOR FUTURE RESEARCH

Given the nature of this investigation consisting of a combination of studies, there are a wide variety of ways to expand or refine this research, even just in responding to the initial questions that motivated this effort, let alone others that have emerged.

One obvious path is to replicate this investigation or an expanded version of it with all of its components, in another state such as California, New York or Florida which has significant Latino population, presence and influence. Researchers could at least begin with a thorough review of any state's official curriculum standards for U.S. history and/or other social studies courses.

Here in Texas, researchers could use our methods to review all of the currently adopted textbooks and complete a detailed assessment as to their individual strengths and weaknesses regarding Latino and minority representation. This could be useful to classroom teachers and administrators who make decisions about book purchases for the district or the classroom.

Using our methods and instruments, many more focus groups could be convened in Texas and other states and certainly more individual interviews could be conducted with U.S. history teachers as well. Based on the themes, issues, and factors which have emerged from this investigation, a survey could be developed and disseminated widely through four to six states with the largest Latino population, and also in states wherein that population is growing at a fast rate. The results of these findings, with all their possible discoveries under statistical analyses, would be both fascinating and quite useful for educational policy, curriculum development, teacher training, and targeted advocacy and activism.

Focusing on the structural impediments to Latino inclusion, more research could be conducted on the extent to which Latinos are represented in the teaching of U.S. history at public and private colleges and universities, especially those with a reputation for diversity and/or with significant numbers of Latino students. Research should also be conducted to determine the extent to which teacher training and certification programs in academia are preparing teachers with the adequate knowledge, skills and attitudes to effectively instruct Latino or other students of color.

Finally, similar methods to those used in this investigation could be utilized to research the quantity and quality of Latino representation in the Language Arts curriculum from early childhood to secondary levels in both textbooks and ancillary materials, such as trade books and computer resources.

There are certainly other research efforts that can derive methodologies, instruments, and deeper understandings generated from this investigation. If despite its limitations, this research effort could inspire more serious investigation on these pivotal topics and issues, then it would have achieved an even higher purpose than originally intended.

POLICY RECOMMENDATIONS

When it comes to history education in Texas, as in every other state, there are many influential actors and institutions, some officially sanctioned, others self-appointed. Below in bullet format, are some policy recommendations for key actors and institutions that could contribute to resolving this problem of Latino exclusion in the teaching of U.S. history.

Also included in this book is Appendix I, a Resource Bibliography on U.S. Latino History, intended as a useful and relevant listing of books and articles for further reading on the Latino experience in America.

Texas Education Agency

- Convene a panel of academics and teachers to revise and rewrite portions of the TEKS so as to specify items of significance related to Latinos in history and social studies.
- Articulate clearly in the mission statement and in the education code, and apply consistently through the TEKS and the standardized tests, that one of the goals of history and social studies education is

to foster increased understanding of all racial and ethnic groups and their pivotal roles in our history.

Textbook Publishers

- Continue to improve on the quantity and quality of information, questions, exercises, and projects related to Latinos in textbooks as well as in ancillary materials.
- Incorporate more Latino perspectives through speeches, letters, biographies, works of literature and art, or any other primary and authentic secondary sources.

Academic Historians and Teacher Educators

- Take an interest in how history and social studies are taught in the public school classroom and actively participate by bringing into public testimony the benefit of their wider knowledge and deeper understanding.
- Become informed through a variety of media about the realities and significance of Latinos in the history, culture, and society of our nation, and share this information, and their insights from it, with their students.
- Help ensure that teacher training programs provide an accurate, objective, and thorough background on Latino topics related to each subject area, especially history, social studies and language arts.
- Help ensure that methods and strategies for effective instruction of Latino learners are integral to teacher training courses at Texas colleges and universities.
- Review curriculum, textbooks and ancillary readings used in teaching U.S. history at the college and university level for Latino inclusion, and develop training and resources to facilitate that inclusion at both graduate and undergraduate levels.
- Develop resources and rewards for professors to author more authentic, accessible, objective, and interesting U.S. history textbooks for public schools in Texas and the nation.
- Encourage, facilitate and fund academic research on issues related to teacher education, social studies teaching, and the integration of Latinos into the public school curriculum.

Classroom Teachers

- Educate themselves about Latino history and culture through books, films, drama, art, and a variety of media and share the most useful and authentic information with their students.
- Develop innovative and interesting methods of engaging students with aspects of the Latino experience so that students can gain understanding about what is universal and what is unique about that experience.
- Attend workshops, conferences and other training and professional venues to widen their horizons and improve the quality of their teaching about the Latino experience.
- Having developed their skills and obtained significant information, teachers should find formal and informal ways of sharing these with their colleagues.
- Become advocates and activists for disseminating objective and authentic information about Latinos in their campus, district and community, especially in collaboration with colleagues and with the school library and public library systems.

Appendix A
Four Levels of TEKS

Four Levels of TEKS

Level 1: Individual. The specific name of an individual is mentioned,
i.e., Martin Luther King

Level 2: Group. The group is specified by name, i.e., Cherokee or Native
Americans

Level 3: Event. An event, issue, concept is included which implies presence
of a group, i.e., Mexican American War, Emancipation Proclamation,
Trail of Tears

Level 4: Category. The group is implied categorically, i.e. "racial minority
groups" or "immigrants"

Table 1: U.S. History TEKS through Reconstruction

	Individual	Group	Event	Category	Totals
African American	1	1	7	3	12
American Indian	0	1	1	3	5
Latino-Hispanic	0	0	2	4	6

Table 2: U.S. History TEKS From Reconstruction to the Present

	Individual	Group	Event	Category	Totals
African American	3	0	3	5	11
American Indian	0	0	1	4	5
Latino-Hispanic	0	0	4	6	10

Table 3: Both High School and Grade 8 U.S. History TEKS

	Individual	Group	Event	Category	Totals
African American	4	1	10	8	23
American Indian	0	1	2	7	10
Latino-Hispanic	0	0	6	10	16

Appendix B
Textbook Tables

Table 1: Garraty/Holt R&W
Sentences by Topic & Hispanic National Origin

Topics	H/L	MA	PR	CA	Totals
1: Why Imm	0	5	1	1	7
2: When/Where	3	9	1	2	15
3: Prblms/Accmp	35	32	6	5	78
4: Events/Issues	21	12	5	4	42
5: Chrcts/Exprns	15	43	31	2	91
6: Leaders	0	27	5	0	32
7: Other Exprns	0	0	0	0	0
Totals by Origin	74	128	49	14	265

Table 2: Davidson/Prentice Hall
Sentences by Topic & Hispanic National Origin

Topics	H/L	MA	PR	CA	Totals
1: Why Imm	1	7	0	1	9
2: When/Where	0	24	6	2	32
3: Prblms/Accmp	20	20	0	10	50
4: Events/Issues	7	17	4	0	28
5: Chrcts/Exprns	26	90	6	2	124
6: Leaders	0	132	1	0	133
7: Other Exprns	0	0	0	0	0
Totals by Origin	54	290	17	15	376

Table 3: Berkin et al/Scott Foresman
Sentences by Topic & Hispanic National Origin

Topics	H/L	MA	PR	CA	Totals
1: Why Imm	0	7	0	0	7
2: When/Where	6	5	2	0	13
3: Prblms/Accmp	11	20	0	0	31
4: Events/Issues	10	7	8	0	25
5: Chrcts/Exprns	14	58	6	1	79
6: Leaders	0	21	4	0	25
7: Other Exprns	0	0	0	0	0
Totals by Origin	41	118	20	1	180

Appendix C

Interview Questions

Experience

1. What part of U.S. history are you currently teaching?
2. What other courses or classes are you currently teaching as well?
3. How many years have you been teaching U.S. history? Social Studies?
4. What other social studies courses have you taught in the past?

Conditions

5. To what extent do you have ready access to all the materials and technology you need to teach?
6. What approximate percentage of your classroom students demonstrate an interest in learning history?
7. To what extent does the required or adopted textbooks serve as a valuable resource in your teaching?
8. Is the U.S. history curriculum provided by your school district well designed?
9. A. Does the TEKS provide a sound framework for the teaching of U.S. history?
   B. What effect does or will the TAAS test have on your teaching of U.S. history?
10. To what extent do your administrators provide you with the support required to do your job well?
11. Are you satisfied with the opportunities offered by your school and/or district for professional development?

Course Content

12. A. What eras, events, individuals, developments, etc. do you prefer, or enjoy teaching about the most?
    B. Why?
13. A. What content or elements of the curriculum are not to your liking, preference, or enjoy teaching about the least?
    B. Why?
14. A. What would you like to teach, cover, include in the curriculum, which, for whatever reasons, you cannot cover in class?
    B. What prevents you from covering this material in your class now?
15. A. Of all the content you have to cover, what would you skip, eliminate, or spend less time on, if you had a choice?
    B. Why?
16. A. If you had the power to decide, what overall or specific changes would you make regarding the content covered in your course?
    B. Why?
    C. What's preventing you from adopting or implementing these changes now?

Ultimate Goals

17. What personal satisfaction do you obtain from teaching U.S. history?
18. What do you want your students to gain from your course?
19. Why is it important for students to learn what you have to teach them?
20. Had you the power, what overall changes would you make in the teaching of U.S. history and why?
21. Is there anything else you would like to say regarding the teaching of U.S. history?

Appendix D
Focus Group Questions

1. What eras, events, individuals, developments, etc. do you prefer, or enjoy teaching about the most?   Why?
2. What content or elements of the curriculum are not to your liking, preference, or enjoy teaching about the least?   Why?
3. What would you like to teach, cover, include in the curriculum, which, for whatever reasons, you cannot cover in class?
3P. What effect will the TAKS state standardized test have on the curriculum content and your teaching?
4. What prevents you from covering the material or engaging in the activities you would like in your class?
5. [Not Asked] ~~Of all the content you have to cover, what would you skip, eliminate, or spend less time on, if you had a choice? Why?~~ (ALREADY ANSWERED)
6. If you had the power to decide, what overall or specific changes would you make regarding the content covered in your course? Why?
7. What's preventing you from adopting or implementing these changes now?
7P. What are the effects or advantages and disadvantages of block scheduling?
8A. To what extent do the required or adopted textbooks serve as a valuable resource in your teaching?
8B. How about the content of the textbook itself . . . What's your opinion about the content, and how effectively that content is covered?
9. Do the TEKS provide a sound framework for the teaching of U.S. history?

10. What effect does the TAKS test have on your teaching of U.S. history?

11. How does the capacity, interest level, or other characteristics of your students influence your choice of content?

12. [Not Asked] ~~What do you want your students to gain from your course?~~ (NOT ESSENTIAL)

13. [Not Asked] ~~How many (what approximate percentage) of your students demonstrate an interest in learning history at the beginning of the course? How many at the end?~~ (NOT ESSENTIAL)

14. What conditions or factors help or hinder your ability to adequately cover current events, such as 9–11?

15. [Not Used]~~Had you the power, what other changes would you make in the teaching of U.S. History and Why?~~ (ALREADY ANSWERED)

16. What is it that hinders or helps your ability to adequately cover the role of racial and ethnic minorities in the teaching of US history?

Letter of Intent

Dear Participant:

You are invited to participate in a study whose purpose is to examine the attitudes and perceptions selected United States history teachers have regarding the content of their courses. I am a doctoral student in Curriculum Studies at the University of Texas at Austin. This study fulfills part of the requirements for my doctoral dissertation, and relates to other research I have conducted on history textbooks and on the Texas Essential Knowledge and Skills (TEKS) for secondary social studies.

From this investigation we hope to gain a better understanding of how those who teach U.S. history perceive the content of their courses and the factors which influence the content choices they make. You are being invited because you currently teach U.S. history at the secondary level. You will be one of 12 to 20 history teachers selected to participate in this study. The participants in this study may join one of several focus groups with a demographic cross-section of US history teachers in the Northside I.S.D.

If you decide to participate in this study, our expectation is that you are willing to engage in an open and frank discussion with the moderator and your colleagues, and freely express your opinions, perceptions, preferences and recommendations. We will be audiotaping the focus group session, and will direct participants to use only first names when referring to each other.

The audiotapes themselves will be accessible only to myself, and will be kept in a secure location. The identities of all participants in the audiotape will be kept confidential throughout the process and in the written report which will integrate the findings of this study.

We ask that just prior to engaging in a group discussion, that each participant fill out a brief background sheet and a course content checklist. Neither the name nor the campus of the participant will be requested or recorded in these two documents. The focus group session itself is estimated to last from 60 to 90 minutes. As a token of our appreciation for your time and effort, we would like offer you a gift certificate of $30.00 to Barnes & Nobles.

You are under no obligation to participate in this study. Your decision to participate or not will have no affect on your future relations with the University of Texas at Austin or Northside ISD. If you have any questions, please ask me now; or if your questions should later arise, reach me at 210–521–2348 or at jnpapr@aol.com You could also contact my faculty sponsor, Dr. Mary Black, at 512–232–3528 or at msblack@mail.utexas.edu. We will be happy to answer any questions you have or listen to your comments.

Please keep this copy for your reference.

Julio Noboa, Doctoral Student
Department of Curriculum and Instruction
College of Education
University of Texas at Austin

Middle School U.S. History Checklist

Please mark next to each name or term either an "a," "b" or "c" regarding its place in your course curriculum:
a=always taught   b=sometimes covered   c=not covered

INDIVIDUALS, GROUPS AND ORGANIZATIONS

___William Penn	___George Washington	___Thomas Jefferson
___Benjamin Franklin	___Samuel Adams	___King George III
___Marquis de Lafayette	___Benjamin Benneker	___Thomas Paine
___Patrick Henry	___James Madison	___Alexander Hamilton
___Juan Ponce de Leon	___Christopher Columbus	___Hernán Cortez
___John Adams	___Abigail Adams	___Paul Revere
___Hernando De Soto	___Bernardo de Gálvez	___John Marshall
___Iroquois Confederacy	___Chief Pontiac	___Andrew Jackson
___Thirteen Colonies	___Spanish Colonies	___Cherokee Indians
___Sequoyah	___American political parties	___John C. Calhoun
___Henry David Thoreau	___Native Americans	___Fa. Junípero Serra
___Mexican Americans	___López de Santa Anna	___African Americans
___Henry Clay	___Daniel Webster	___Jefferson Davis
___Ulysses S. Grant	___Robert E. Lee	___Abraham Lincoln
___Benito Juarez	___Frederick Douglass	___Harriet Tubman
___Elizabeth Cady Stanton	___Underground Railroad	___Sojourner Truth
___Simón Bolívar	___Sacajawea	___David G. Farragut

ERAS AND EVENTS

___European Exploration   ___French and Indian War   ___English colonization

___Spanish colonization   ___American Revolution   ___African slave trade

___Treaty of Paris   ___Philadelphia Convention 1787

___War of 1812   ___Trail of Tears   ___Mexican War

___Lewis & Clark Expedition ___abolitionist movement   ___Reconstruction

___Great Awakenings   ___expansionism   ___Reform movement

Battles of: Lexington____/ Concord____/ Saratoga____/ Yorktown____/

Fort Sumpter____Gettysburg____Vicksburg____/

KEY CONCEPTS AND DOCUMENTS

___Mayflower Compact   ___Magna Carta   ___Common Sense

___Declaration of Independence ___U.S. Constitution   ___Bill of Rights

___Articles of Confederation   ___democracy   ___culture

___Federalist Papers   ___mercantalism   ___equality

___representative government   ___urbanization   ___immigration

___free enterprise system   ___industrialization   ___Monroe Doctrine

___Emancipation Proclamation   ___civil disobedience   ___racism

___Gettysburg Address   ___Northwest Ordinance   ___slavery

___separation of powers   ___Manifest Destiny   ___ethnicity

___church & state separation   ___role of religion   ___women's rights

___Treaty of Guadalupe-Hidalgo ___13th, 14th and 15th Amendments

Appendix G:
High School U.S. History Checklist

Please mark next to each name or term either an "a," "b" or "c" regarding its place in your course curriculum:
a=always taught   b=sometimes covered   c=not covered

INDIVIDUALS, GROUPS AND ORGANIZATIONS

___Henry Cabot Lodge

___W.E.B. DuBois

___George Wallace

___Williams Jennings Bryan

___George Marshall

___Martin Luther King, Jr.

___John Steinbeck

___Franklin D. Roosevelt

___Dwight D. Eisenhower

___Richard M. Nixon

___George H. W. Bush

___César Chávez

___Eleanor Roosevelt

___William C. Velasquez

___American Indian Movement

___N.A.T.O.

___the Chicago Seven

___Henry Cabot Lodge

___Eugene Debs

___Pedro Albizu Campos

___Charles A. Lindbergh

___George Patton

___Shirley Chisholm

___Theodore Roosevelt

___Herbert C. Hoover

___John F. Kennedy

___James E. Carter

___William J. Clinton

___Luis Muñoz Marin

___Henry B. Gonzalez

___Lyndon B. Johnson

___N.O.W.

___L.U.L.A.C.

___M.A.L.D.E.F.

___Susan B Anthony

___H. Ross Perot

___Henry Ford

___Douglas MacArthur

___Andrew Carnegie

___Georgia O'Keeffe

___Woodrow Wilson

___Harry S. Truman

___Clarence Darrow

___Ronald W. Reagan

___Malcolm X

___Alex Hailey

___Antonia Pantojas

___Gloria Steinem

___Black Panthers

___C.I.A.

___K.K.K.

ERAS AND EVENTS

___Spanish American War	___Chinese Revolution	___World War I
___World War II	___Civil Rights Movement	___Prohibition
___Progressive Era	___Indian Wars & removal	___Red Scare
___Japanese Amer internment	___the Holocaust	___Watergate
___Cold War	___Vietnam War	___Great Depression
___growth of labor unions	___rise of big business	___Chicano Movement

Battles, invasions, etc.: Argonne Forest____/Midway____/ Normandy____/

Tet Offensive____Bataan March____Bay of Pigs____/

KEY CONCEPTS AND DOCUMENTS

___political parties & machines	___U.S. Expansionism	___industrialization
___atomic weapons	___Wilson's 14 Points	___Truman Doctrine
___Treaty of Versailles	___16th & 17th Amendments	___Marshall Plan
___baby boom	___Civil Rights Act of 1964	___discrimination
___affirmative action	___immigration	___communism
___fascism	___socialism	___imperialism
___Third World	___Sherman Anti-Trust Act	___New Deal
___Open Door Policy	___Dollar Diplomacy	___Social Security
___McCarthyism	___*Brown vs. Bd of Ed.*	___*U.of C. vs. Bakke*
___19th, 24th & 26th Amends	___consumerism	___the internet

Appendix H:
Checklist of Critiques

PP#	Who	Themes, Topics, Issues & Concerns	Accuracy	Bias	Content

Resource Bibliography on U.S. Latino History

This bibliography provides a selected listing of books and articles on Latino history and heritage in the United States. Although not intended to be updated nor comprehensive, it is a useful resource for secondary and university level students and educators who seek to expand their knowledge and understanding of the U.S. Latino experience.

Acuña, Rodolfo. (1988). *Occupied America: A history of Chicanos.* Third Ed. New York: Harper Collins.

Algarín, M. & Piñero, M. (1975). *Nuyorican poetry: An anthology of Puerto Rican words and feelings.* New York: William Morrow & Co.

Alonzo, Armando C. (1998). *Tejano legacy: Rancheros and settlers in South Texas, 1734–1900.* Albuquerque, NM: University of New Mexico Press.

Allsup, Carl. (1982). *The American G.I. Forum: Origins and evolution.* Austin, TX: University of Texas Press.

Anaya, Rudolfo A. & Lomeli, Francisco A. (1991). *Aztlan: Essays on the Chicano homeland* (Reprint ed.). Albuquerque, NM: University of New Mexico Press.

Anzaldúa, Gloria. (1999). *Borderlands/La frontera: The new mestiza.* Second Edition. San Francisco, CA: Aunt Lute Books.

Balido, Giselle. (2001). *Cubantime: A celebration of Cuban life in America.* New York: Silver Lining Books.

Barrera, Mario. (1979). *Race and class in the Southwest.* Notre Dame, IN: University of Notre Dame Press.

Bercht, F., Brodsky, E., Farmer, J.A., and Taylor, D. (Eds.). (1997). *Taíno: Pre-Columbian art and culture from the Caribbean.* New York: Monacelli Press & El Museo Del Barrio.

Black, George. (1988). *The good neighbors: How the United States wrote the history of Central America and the Caribbean.* New York: Pantheon Books.

Boswell, T.D. & Curtis, J.R. (1983). *The Cuban-American experience: Culture, images, and perspectives.* Totowa, NJ: Rowman & Allanheld.

Burns, Walter Noble. (1999). *The Robin Hood of El Dorado: The saga of Joaquin Murrieta, famous outlaw of California's age of gold.* Albuquerque, NM: University of New Mexico Press.

Cabán, P.A., Carrusco, J., Cruz, B., & Garcia, J. (Eds.). (1994). *The Latino experience in U.S. history.* Paramus, NJ: Globe Fearon.

Campos, Pedro A. (1993). *Writings of Pedro Albizu Campos.* New York: Gordon Press Publishers.

Carr, Raymond. (1984). *Puerto Rico: A colonial experiment.* New York: Vintage.

Chavez, J. (1984). *The lost land: The Chicano image of the Southwest.* Albuquerque, NM: University of New Mexico Press.

Cockcroft, James D. (1995). *Latinos in the making of the United States.* New York: Franklin Watts.

Coonrod Martinez, Elizabeth. (1995). *Coming to America: The Mexican American experience.* Brookfield, CN: The Milbrook Press, Inc.

Crawford, James. (1992). *Hold your tongue: Bilingualism and the politics of "English Only."* New York: Addison-Wesley Publishing.

De Genova, Nicholas, et al. (2003). *Latino crossings: Mexicans, Puerto Ricans, and the politics of race and citizenship.* New York: Routledge.

de la Garza, Rodolfo O., Bean, Frank D., Bonjean, Charles M., Romo, Ricardo, and Avarez, Ricardo. (Eds.). (1985). *The Mexican American experience.* Austin, TX: The University of Texas Press.

De La Peña, José Enrique. (1997). *With Santa Anna in Texas: A personal narrative of the revolution.* (Carmen Perry, Trans.) Expanded Edition. College Station, TX: Texas A&M University Press.

De León, Arnoldo. (1983). *They called them greasers: Anglo attitudes towards Mexicans in Texas, 1821–1900.* Austin, TX: University of Texas Press.

———. (1993). *Mexican Americans in Texas: A brief history.* Arlington Heights, IL: Harlan Davidson, Inc.

de Varona, Frank. (1989). *Hispanics in U.S. history.* (Vols. 1&2). Englewood Globe Book Co.

———. (1996). *Latino literacy: A complete guide to our Hispanic history and culture.* New York: Henry Holt & Co.

Delgado, R. & Stefancic, J. (Eds.) (1998). *The Latino Condition: A Critical Reader.* New York: New York University Press.

Delgado Votaw, Carmen. (1995). *Puerto Rican women.* Washington, DC: Lisboa Associates, Inc.

Department of Defense. (1983). *Hispanics in America's Defense.* Office of Deputy Assistant Secretary of Defense for Equal Opportunity and Safety Policy.

Duany, Jorge. (2002). *The Puerto Rican nation on the move: Identities on the island and in the United States.* Chapel Hill, NC: University of North Carolina Press.

Escamilla, Kathy. (1996.) Incorporating Mexican American history and culture into the social studies classroom. ERIC: ED 393645.

Fernandez, Ronald. (1992). *The disenchanted island: Puerto Rico and the United States in the twentieth century.* Westport, CN: Praeger Press.

————. (1994). *Prisoners of colonialism: The struggle for justice in Puerto Rico.* Monroe, Maine: Common Courage Press.

Fernández-Shaw, Carlos. (1991). *The Hispanic presence in North America: From 1492 to today.* New York: Facts On File, Inc.

Flores, Juan. (1993). *Divided borders: Essays on Puerto Rican identity.* Houston, TX: Arte Publico Press.

————. (2000). *From bomba to hip-hop: Puerto Rican culture and Latino identity.* New York: Columbia University Press.

Flores, William V. & Benmayor, Rina. (1997). *Latino cultural citizenship: Claiming identity, space, and rights.* Boston: Beacon Press.

Fox, Geoffrey. (1996). *Hispanic nation: Culture, politics, and the construction of identity.* Secaucus, NJ: Carol Publishing.

Freedman, Russell. (2001). *In the days of the vaqueros: America's first true cowboys.* New York: Clarion Books.

Garcia, Eugene E. (2001). *Hispanic education in the United States: Raices y alas.* New York: Rowman & Littlefield Publishers.

Glab, Edward, Jr. (1981) *Latin American cultural studies: Information and materials for teaching about Latin America.* Austin, TX: University of Texas, Institute of Latin American Studies. ED 216943.

Gonzales, Rodolpho "Corky." (2001). *Message to Aztlan: Selected writings.* (Hispanic Civil Rights). Houston, TX: Arte Publico Press.

Gonzalez, José Luis. (1993). *Puerto Rico: The four-storeyed country.* (Gerald Guinness, Trans.). New York: Markus Wiener Publishing. Gonzalez, Juan.

Gonzalez, Juan. (2000). *Harvest of empire: A history of Latinos in America.* New York: Viking.

Gutierrez, José Angel. (1999). *The making of a Chicano militant: Lessons from Cristal.* (Wisconsin Studies in Autobiography) Madison, WI: University of Wisconsin Press.

Haney-Lopez, Ian F. (2003). *Racism on trial: The Chicano fight for justice.* New York: Belknap Press.

Harris, W.W. (2001). *Puerto Rico's fighting 65th U.S. Infantry.* Novato, CA: Presidio Press, Inc.

Haslip-Viera, Gabriel. (Ed.) (2001). *Taíno revival: Critical perspectives on Puerto Rican identity and cultural politics.* Princeton, NJ: Markus Wiener Publishers.

Hauptly, Denis J. (1991). *Puerto Rico: An unfinished story.* New York: Atheneum.

Helly, M. & Courgeon, R. (1996). *Montezuma and the Aztecs.* New York: Henry Holt and Company.

Jiménez, Carlos M. (1994). *The Mexican American heritage.* Second Edition. Berkeley, CA: TQS Publications.

Johnson, Benjamin Heber. (2003). *Revolution in Texas: How a forgotten rebellion and its bloody suppression turned Mexicans into Americans.* Princeton, NJ: Yale University Press.

Johnson, John J. (1980). *Latin America in caricature.* Austin, TX: University of Texas Press.

Kanellos, N. and Pérez, C. (1995). *Chronology of Hispanic American history.* New York: Gale Research Inc.

Kanellos, Nicolás. (1997). *Hispanic firsts: 500 years of extraordinary achievement.* New York: Visible Ink Press.
———. (1997). *The Hispanic literary companion.* New York: Visible Ink Press.
———. (1998). *Thirty million strong: Reclaiming the Hispanic image in American culture.* Golden, CO: Fulcrum Publishing.
LaFarelle, Lorenzo G. (1992). *Bernardo De Gálvez: Hero of the American revolution.* Austin, TX: Eakin Press.
Lattin, V.E., Hinojosa, R., & Keller, G.D. (1988). *Tomás Rivera, 1935–1984: The man and his work.* Tempe, AZ: Bilingual Review/Press.
Levy, Jacques E. (1975). *César Chávez: Autobiography of La Causa.* New York: W.W. Norton & Co.
Lewis, Gordon K. (1963). *Puerto Rico: Freedom and power in the Caribbean.* New York: Harper & Row.
Lopez Tijerina, Reies. (2001). *They called me "King Tiger": My struggle for the land and our rights* (Hispanic Civil Rights) (José Angel Gutierrez, Trans.). Houston, TX: Arte Publico Press.
Marin, Cheech. (2002). *Chicano visions: American painters on the verge.* New York: Little, Brown and Company.
Martí, José. (1966). *Martí on the U.S.A.* (Luis A. Baralt, Trans. and Introduction). Carbondale, IL: Southern Illinois University Press.
Martinez, Elizabeth. (Ed.). (1991). *500 years of Chicano history in pictures.* Albuquerque, NM: SouthWest Organizing Project.
Matos-Rodriguez, F.V. & Hernandez, P. J. (2001). *Pioneros: Puerto Ricans in New York City 1896–1948* (Bilingual ed.). (Images of America). New York: Arcadia Publishing.
Matovina, Timothy, M. (1995). *The Alamo remembered: Tejano account and perspectives.* Austin, TX: University of Texas Press.
Meier, Matt S., & Gutierrez, Margo. (2000). *Encyclopedia of the Mexican American civil rights movement.* Westport, CN: Greenwood Press.
Meléndez, Edwin & Meléndez, Edgardo. (1993). *Colonial dilemma: Critical perspectives on contemporary Puerto Rico.* Boston, MA: South End Press.
Melendez, Miguel. (2003). *We took the streets: Fighting for Latino rights with the Young Lords.* New York: St. Martin's Press.
Montejano, David. (1987). *Anglos and Mexicans in the making of Texas, 1836–1986.* Austin, TX: University of Texas Press.
Morales Carrión, Arturo. (1983). *Puerto Rico: A Political and cultural history.* New York: W. W. Norton & Company.
Morales, Ed. (2002). *Living in Spanglish: The Search for Latino identity in America.* New York: St. Martin's Press.
Munson, Sammye. (1989). *Our Tejano heroes: Outstanding Mexican-Americans in Texas.* Austin, TX: Panda Books.
Murillo, Mario. (2001). *Islands of resistance: Puerto Rico, Vieques, and U.S. policy.* New York: Seven Stories Press.
Novas, Himilce. (1994). *Everything you need to know about Latino history.* New York: Penguin Books.

Ochoa, George. (2001). *Atlas of Hispanic-American history*. New York:Checkmark Books/Facts On File, Inc.

Olmos, E.J., Ybarra, L. & Monterrey, M. (1999) *Americanos: Latino life in the United States*. New York: Little, Brown & Company.

Padilla, Felix. (1985). *Latino ethnic consciousness: The case of Mexican-Americans and Puerto Ricans in Chicago*. Notre Dame, IN: Notre Dame University Press.

Pantoja, Antonia. (2002). *Memoir of a visionary: Antonia Pantoja*. Houston, TX: Arte Público Press.

Phelps de Córdova, Loretta. (1993). *Five centuries in Puerto Rico: Portraits and eras*. San Juan, P.R.: Publishing Resources, Inc.

Pitt, Leonard. (1999). *Decline of the Californios: A social history of the Spanish-Speaking Californias, 1846–1890*. Los Angeles, CA: University of California Press.

Portales, Marco. (2000). *Crowding out Latinos: Mexican Americans in the public consciousness*. Philadelphia, PA: Temple University Press.

Ramirez III, Manuel, & Castañeda, Afredo. (1974). *Cultural democracy, bicognitive development, and education*. New York: Academic Press.

Rosales, Arturo F. (1997). *Chicano! The history of the Mexican American civil rights movement*. Houston, TX: Arte Público Press.

Rebolledo, T.D., and Rivero, E.S. (Eds.) (1993). *Infinite divisions: An anthology of Chicana literature*. Tempe, AZ: University of Arizona Press.

Rendon Lozano, Ruben. (1985). *Viva Tejas: The Story of Tejanos*. San Antonio, TX: Alamo Press.

Ribes Tovar, Federico. (1971). *Albizu Campos: Puerto Rican revolutionary* (Anthony Rawlings, Trans.). New York: Plus Ultra.

Rivas-Rodriquez, Maggie. (Ed.) (2005). *Mexican Americans and World War II*. Austin, TX: University of Texas Press.

Rivera, Jose A. (2002). *The political thought of Luis Muñoz Marin*. New York: Xlibris Corporation.

Roberts, John Storm. (1999). *The Latin tinge: The Impact of Latin American music on the United States*. Second Edition. New York: Oxford University Press.

Rodriquez, Clara E. (1989). *Puerto Ricans: Born in the U.S.A.* Boston: Unwin Hyman.

———. (Ed.). (1997). *Latin looks: Images of Latinas and Latinos in the U.S. media*. Boulder, CO: Westview Press.

Rodriquez, C. & Sánchez Korrol, V. (1980). *Historical perspectives on Puerto Rican survival in the U.S.* Princeton, NJ: Markus Wiener.

Rosales, Rodolfo. (2000). *The illusion of inclusion: The untold political story of San Antonio*. Austin, TX: University of Texas Press.

Rubio, Abel. (1986). *Stolen heritage: A Mexican-American's rediscovery of his family's lost land grant*. Austin, TX: Eakin Press.

Ruiz, Vicki L. (1987, February). Teaching Chicano/American history: Goals and methods. *The History Teacher*. 20 (2), 167–177.

Salazar Davis, Norma. (1991). Recovering the Hispanic past: Historiography in a void. Paper. Annual Meeting of American Educational Research Association, Chicago, IL, April 6. ED 333092

Samora, Julian. (1993). *A History of the Mexican-American people.* Notre Dame, IN: University of Notre Dame.

Sandos, James A. (1992). *Rebellion in the borderlands: Anarchism and the Plan of San Diego, 1904–1923.* Norman, OK: University of Oklahoma Press.

Sanchez, George. (1995). *Becoming Mexican American: Ethnicity, culture and identity in Chicano Los Angeles, 1900–1945.* New York: Oxford University Press.

Sánchez Korrol, Virginia E. (1983). *From colonia to community: The History of Puerto Ricans in New York City.* Berkeley: University of California Press.

Santiago, Roberto. (Ed.) (1995). *Boricuas: Influential Puerto Rican writings.* New York: Ballantine Books.

Sedillo Lopez, Antoinette. (Ed.). (1995). *Historical themes and identity (Latinos in the United States: History, law and perspective).* Garland Publishing.

———. (Ed.). (1999). *Latina issues: Fragments of Historia (ella) (herstory)* Garland Publishing.

Sepulveda, Juan. (2004). *The life & times of Willie Velásquez.* (The Hispanic Civil Rights Series) Houston, TX: Arte Publico Press.

Schon, Isabel. (1980). *A Hispanic heritage: A guide to juvenile books about Hispanic people and cultures.* Metuchen, NJ: The Scarecrow Press.

Shorris, Earl. (1992). *Latinos: A biography of the people.* New York: Avon Books.

Stavans, Ilan. (1995). *The Hispanic condition: Reflections on culture and identity in America.* New York: Harper Collins.

Stavans, Ilan & Augenbraum, Harold. (Eds.). (1993). *Growing up Latino: Memoirs and stories.* New York: Houghton Mifflin.

Stevens-Arroyo, Antonio M. (1974) *The political philosophy of Pedro Albizu Campos: Its theory and practice.* New York: New York University, Ibero-American Language and Area Center.

Suro, Roberto. (1998). *Strangers among us: How Latino immigration is transforming America.* New York: Knopf.

Talgen, D. and Kamp, J. (1996). *¡Latinas! women of achievement.* New York: Visible Ink Press.

Tatum, Charles. (Ed.) (1990). *Mexican American literature.* Dallas, TX: Harcourt Brace Jovanovich.

Tecihtzin. (1996). *Chía: A powerful recuerdo.* San Antonio, TX: Tochtli Publishing.

Thonhoff, Robert H. (1981). *The Texas connection with the American Revolution.* Austin, TX: Eakin Press.

Torres, Andres & Velazquez, Jose E. (Eds.). (1998). *The Puerto Rican movement: Voices from the diaspora* (Puerto Rican Studies). Temple University Press.

Turner, Faythe. (Ed.). (1991). *Puerto Rican writers at home in the USA.* Seattle, WA: Open Hand Publishing, Inc.

Trias Monge, José. (1997). *Puerto Rico: The trials of the oldest colony in the world.* New Haven, CN: Yale University Press.

Trueba, Enrique. (1999). *Latinos unidos: From cultural diversity to the politics of solidarity.* New York: Rowman and Littlefield.

Venable, Fay. (1985). *North to the Rio Grande: Lorenzo de Zavala: First vice-president of the Republic of Texas.* Austin, TX: Eakin Press.

Vigil, Ernesto B. (1999). *The Crusade for Justice: Chicano militancy and the goven-ment's war on dissent.* Madison, WI: University of Wisconsin Press.

Wagenheim, Kal & Jimenez de Wagenheim, Olga. (Eds.). (1993). *The Puerto Ricans: A documentary history.* Princeton, NJ: Markus Weiner.

Zamora, E., Orozco, C., & Rocha, R. (Eds.). (2000). *Mexican Americans in Texas history.* Austin, TX: Texas State Historical Society.

References

Apple, M.W., & Christian-Smith, L.K. (Eds.) (1991). *The politics of the textbook.* New York: Routledge.

Arries, Jonathan F. (1994). Decoding the social studies production of Chicano history. *Equity & Excellence in Education.* April. 27 (1), 37–44.

Banks, James A. (1969) A content analysis of the Black American in textbooks. *Social Education,* December, 954–63.

———. (1997). Multicultural education: Characteristics and goals. In J. Banks & McGee Banks, C.A. *Multicultural education: issues and perspectives.* Boston, MA: Allyn and Bacon, 3–31.

———. (1999). *An introduction to multicultural education* (2nd ed.). Second edition. Boston, MA: Allyn and Bacon.

Beatty, A.S., et al. (1996). *NAEP 1994 U.S. history report card: Findings of the National Assessment of Educational Progress.* Washington D.C: National Center for Education Statistics, U.S. Dept. of Education. April.

Ben-Peretz, M. (1990). *The teacher-curriculum encounter: Freeing teachers from the tyranny of texts.* Albany, New York : State University of New York Press.

Berkin, Carol, et al. (1992). *American voices: A history of the United States, Volume II: 1865 to the present.* Glenview, IL : Scott Foresman.

Bernal, Joe. (1997). Everyone had a fair say in new class curriculum. *San Antonio Express-News,* August 12.

Boyer, Paul & Stuckey, Sterling. (2003). *The American nation.* Austin, TX: Holt, Rinehart and Winston.

Canning, C. and Noboa, J. (1997). White teachers in a multicultural society. *Association of Teacher Educators Annual Conference.* Washington, D.C., February 17.

Canning, C., Noboa, J., and Salazar-Guenther, M. (2002) Reflecting Latino culture in our classrooms: A quick start for teachers. *Association of Teacher Educators Annual Conference.* Denver, CO. February.

Cayton, Perry, Reed & Winkler. (2003). *America: Pathways to the present.* Englewood Cliffs, NJ: Prentice Hall.

Children Now (1998). *A different world: Children's perceptions of race and class in the media.* Oakland CA: Children Now.

Christian Science Monitor. (2001). Hispanics spread to hinterlands. March 26.

Committee on the Study of Teaching Materials in Intergroup Relations. (1949). *Intergroup relations in teaching materials.* Washington D.C.: American Council on Education.

Cook, Kay K. (1985). *Latin American studies.* ERIC Digest no. 19. ERIC Clearinghouse for Social Studies/Social Sciences Education, September. ED 264161.

Cortés, Carlos E. (1997). Chicanas in film: History of an image. in Clara E. Rodriquez, (Ed.) *Latin looks: Images of Latinas and Latinos in the U.S. Media.* Boulder, CO: Westview Press., 121–141.

———. (2000). *The children are watching: How the media teach about diversity.* New York: Teachers College Press.

Cruz, Bárbara C. (2002). Don Juan and rebels under palm trees: Depictions of Latin Americans in US history textbooks. *Critique of Anthropology.* Vol 22(3).

Davidson, J.W., Lytle, M.H. and Stoff, M.B. (1992). *American journey: The quest for liberty since 1865.* Englewood Cliffs, NJ: Prentice Hall.

Delgado, R. & Stefancic, J. (2001). *Critical race theory: An introduction.* New York: New York University Press.

de Varona, Frank. (1989). *Hispanics must be included in our textbooks.* National Association of Bilingual Administrators Conference, Miami, Fl, May 11. ERIC ED 314318.

D'Souza, Dinesh. (1991). *Illiberal education.* New York: Free Press. Elbaz, F. (1981). The teachers' practical knowledge. *Curriculum Inquiry,* 11 (1), 43–71.

Eslinger, M. & Superka, D. (1982). Social studies teachers. in *The current state of social studies.* Boulder, CO: Social Science Consortium.

Fawcett, V. & Hawke, S. (1982). Instructional practice in social studies. in *The current state of social studies.* Boulder, CO: Social Science Consortium.

Fern, Edward F. (2001). *Advanced focus group research.* Thousand Oaks, CA: Sage Publications.

Fitzgerald, Frances. (1980) *America revisited.* New York: Vintage Books.

Fleming, Dan B. (1982) Latin America and the United States: What do U. S. history books tell us? *The Social Studies.* July/August. (73), 168–171.

Garcia, Jesus. (1980). Hispanic perspective: Textbooks and other curricular materials. *The History Teacher.* November. 14 (1), 105–120.

———. (1993). The changing image of ethnic groups in textbooks. *Phi Delta Kappan.* September. 75 (1), 29–35.

Garcia, J. & Goebel, J. (1985) A comparative study of the portrayal of Black Americans in selected U.S. history textbooks. *Negro Educational Review,* July/October, 118–127.

Garraty, John. (1992). *The story of America, Vol. 2: 1865 to the present.* Austin, TX: Holt, Rinehart and Winston.

Gay, Geneva. (1994). *A synthesis of scholarship in multicultural education.* Urban Education Monograph Series. Seattle: NCREL Urban Education Program.

Gibson, Margaret A. (1989). School persistence versus dropping out: A comparative perspective. in H.T. Trueba, G. Spindler & L. Spindler (Eds.) *What do anthropologists have to say about dropouts?* New York: The Falmer Press.

Glab, Edward, Jr. (1981) Latin American cultural studies: Information and materials for teaching about Latin America (Rev. ed.). Austin: University of Texas, Institute of Latin American Studies. ED 216943.

Glazer, Nathan & Ueda, Reed. (1983) *Ethnic groups in history textbooks.* Washington D.C.: Ethics and Public Policy Center. 60.

Gonzalez, Juan. (2000). *Harvest of empire: A history of Latinos in America.* New York: Viking.

Gonzales, P. & Rodriquez, R. (1998) Justice, truth, part of human rights. *San Antonio Express-News,* December 7.

Hirsch, E.D., Jr. (1987) *Cultural literacy: What every American needs to know.* Boston: Houghton Mifflin.

Hoholik, Suzanne. (1998). State gets praise for TEKS plan. *San Antonio Express-News,* February 24.

Jarolimek, John (1981). The social studies: An overview. in H. Mehlinger and O. Davis (Eds.). *The social studies 80th yearbook of the National Society for the Study of Education.* Chicago: National Society for the Study of Education.

Kane, Michael B. (1970). *Minorities in Textbooks.* Chicago: Quadrangle Books.

Krueger, Richard A. (1998). *Analyzing and reporting focus group results.* (Focus Group Kit 6). Thousand Oaks, CA: Sage Publications.

Ladson-Billings, G. (1999). Just what is critical race theory, and what's it doing in a nice field like education? in L. Parker, D. Deyle, and S. Villenas (Eds.). *Race is . . . race isn't: Critical race theory and qualitative studies in education.* Boulder, CO: Westview Press.

Lapp, M.S., Grigg, W.S., & Tay-Lim, B.S.H. (2002) *The Nation's report card: U.S. history 2001.* Washington DC: National Center for Education Statistics, U.S. Department of Education

Lerner, R., Nagai, A.K., & Rothman, S. (1995) *Molding the good citizen: The politics of high school history texts.* Westport, Connecticut: Praeger.

Levine, L. (1996). *The opening of the American mind: Canons, culture, and history.* Boston: Beacon Press.

Lietman, R., Binns, K., & Steinberg, A. (Eds.). (1996). *Students voice their opinions on: Learning about multiculturalism.* Part IV. The Metropolitan Life Survey of The American Teacher. New York: Louis Harris & Associates, Inc.

Little, Judith. (1989). Conditions of professional development in secondary schools. *1989 AERA Annual Meeting.*

Madriz, Esther. (2000). Focus groups in feminist research. in N.K. Denzin & Y.S. Lincoln. (Eds.). *Handbook of qualitative research.* Thousand Oaks, CA: Sage Publications, Inc., 835–850.

Marcus, Lloyd. (1961). *The Treatment of Minorities in Secondary School Textbooks.* New York: Anti-Defamation League of B'nai B'rith.

Mckee, Saundra. (1988). Impediments to implementing critical thinking. *Social Education.* 52 (6).

Morgan, David L. (1988). *Focus groups as qualitative research* (2nd ed.). Thousand Oaks, CA: Sage Publications.

Morrisett, Irving (1981). The needs of the future and the constraints of the past. in H. Mehlinger and O. Davis (Eds.). *The social studies 80th yearbook of the*

National Society for the Study of Education. Chicago: National Society for the Study of Education.

Nash, G.B. & Crabtree, C. (1996). *National standards for United States history* (Basic Edition). Los Angeles, CA: University of California, National Center for History in the Schools.

Nash, Gary B., Crabtree, C., & Dunn, R.E. (1997) *History on trial: Culture wars and the teaching of the past.* New York: Alfred A. Knoff.

Nash, G.B. & Dunn, R.E. (1995, January). History standards and culture wars. *Social Education.* 59, 5–7.

National Council of La Raza (1997). Hispanics in the media. in Clara E. Rodriquez, (Ed.). *Latin looks: images of Latinas and Latinos in the U.S. media.* Boulder, CO: Westview Press., 21–35

Newman, W.N. (1973). *A study of minority groups and social theory.* New York: Harper & Row.

Nieto, Sonia. (1992). *Affirming diversity: The sociopolitical context of multicultural education.* New York: Longman Publishing Group.

Noboa, Julio. (1991a) Mexican Americans and Hispanics in U.S. history textbooks: Grades 9 to 12. Testimony presented at the Texas Board of Education, Austin. July 9 and November 7.

———. (1991b). The Textbook adoption process in Texas: Social studies and cultural diversity. *Southwestern Social Science Association,* San Antonio, TX. March 30.

———. (1993). Latinos, minorities, and women in literature and history textbooks. *Society for Applied Anthropology,* Menger Hotel, San Antonio, TX. March 10.

———. (1998). Missing pages from the human story: World history according to TEKS. *World History Association of Texas Conference,* Texas Lutheran University. April 4.

———. (1999). Growing up Latino in anglocentric schools: The impact of school and media curricula. Unpublished Manuscript. Spring.

———. (2000a) U.S. history teachers engaging with the content of their teaching. University of Texas at Austin, Spring. Unpublished manuscript.

———. (2000b) Latino presence and perspective in U.S. history textbooks. University of Texas at Austin, Summer. Unpublished manuscript.

———. (2000c) Looking for Latinos in U.S. history TEKS. *First Conference on Curriculum & Pedagogy,* Camp Balcones Springs, Austin, TX. November 10.

———. (2003a) Latinos in the U.S. history textbook adoption process of Texas, 2002. Univesity of Texas at Austin, Spring. Unpublished manuscript.

———. (2003b) What to teach: How U.S. history teachers make content choices. University of Texas at Austin. Summer. Unpublished study.

———. (2005). On the westside: A portrait of Lanier high school during World War II. In Maggie Rivas-Rodriquez. (Ed.), *Mexican Americans and World War II.* Austin, TX: University of Texas Press.

Noboa-Polanco, Julio (1991) *They come to learn: Hispanic immigrant students in Texas.* The Tomás Rivera Center. Trinity University, San Antonio, TX.

Offutt, Robert. (1997). TEKS improved, but students lost best curriculum. *San Antonio Express-News,* August 26.

Patthey-Chavez, G.G. (1993,). High school as an arena for cultural conflict and acculturation for Latino angelinos. *Anthropology and Education Quarterly.* March. 24 (1), 33–60.

Romanowski, Michael H. (1995). American history by the book: Teachers using textbooks. *Annual Meeting of American Educational Research Association* 1995. ERIC ED 396978.

———. (1997). Teachers' lives and beliefs: Influences that shape the U.S. history curriculum. *Annual Meeting of American Educational Research Association* 1997. ERIC ED 409288.

Ramos, Cindy (1997). Debate gets political on school curriculum. *San Antonio Express News,* June 30, p. 8.

Rigberg, B. (1991). What Must Not Be Taught. *Theory and Research in Social Education.* Winter. 19 (1), 14–44.

Ruiz, Vicki L. (1987). Teaching Chicano/American history: goals and methods. *The History Teacher.* February. 20 (2), 167–177.

Salazar Davis, Norma. (1991). Recovering the Hispanic past: Historiography in a void. *Annual Meeting of American Educational Research Association,* Chicago, IL, April 6. ED 333092

Salvucci, Linda K. (1991,). Mexico, Mexicans and Mexican Americans in secondary-school United States history textbooks. *The History Teacher.* February. 24 (2), 203–222.

Sewall, G.T. & Emberling, S.W. (1998). A new generation of history textbooks. *Society.* Nov/Dec. 36 (1), 78–85.

Schlesinger, Arthur M., Jr. (1991). *The disuniting of America: Reflections on a multicultural society.* Knoxville, TN: Whittle Direct Books.

Shaver, James, et al. (1978). An interpretive report of the status of precollege social studies education based on three NSF funded studies. ED 164363.

Simms, Richard L. (1975) Bias in textbooks: Not yet corrected. *Phi Delta Kappan,* November. 201–2.

Sleeter, C.E., Grant, C.A. (1991). Race, class, gender, and disability in current textbooks. in Apple, M.W., & Christian-Smith, L.K. (Eds.) *The Politics of the textbook.* New York: Routledge.

———. (1994). *Making choices for multicultural education* (2nd ed.). New York: Macmillan Publishing Co.

Sobol, Morton J. (1954). An analysis of social studies texts in relation to their treatment of four areas of human relations. Doctoral dissertation, Wayne State University.

Spring, Joel (1997) *Deculturalization and the struggle for equality: A brief history of the education of dominated cultures in the United States* (2nd ed.). New York: McGraw-Hill, Inc.

Stake, Robert, et al. (1978). Case studies in science education. Volume 2. Design, overview, and general findings. ERIC ED 166059.

Stille, Alexander. (1998). The Betrayal of History. *The New York Review of Books.* June 11, 15–20.

Suarez-Orozco, Marcelo M. (1989). *Central American refugees and U.S. high schools: A psychosocial study of motivation and achievement.* Stanford, CA: Stanford University Press.

Swartz, E. (1992). Emancipatory narratives: Rewriting the master script in the school curriculum. *Journal of Negro Education,* 61, 341.

Texas Education Agency. (1992) *Written comments concerning textbooks to be reviewed by the state textbook social studies committee (1992 adoption).* Division of Textbook Administration, Texas Education Agency.

———. (1996). *Social studies: Texas essential knowledge and skills.* (2nd Draft, July 1). Austin, TX: Author.

———. (1997a). Scholars endorse curriculum proposals (Press Release: July 9). Austin, TX: Author.

———. (1997b). *Chapter 113: Texas essential knowledge and skills for social studies.* (September, 1997, Original) Austin, TX: Author.

———. (1997c). *Chapter 113: Texas essential knowledge and skills for social studies.* (Second Reading Final Adoption: Draft, July 2). Austin, TX: Author.

———. (2002a). *Public testimony before the state board of education. Proclomation 2000.* (Textbook Hearing #1). July 17, 2002. Austin, TX: Author.

———. (2002b). *Public hearing on textbooks before the state board of education: September 11, 2002.* Austin, TX: Author.

Thomas, Jeffrey. (1992). Teachers of U.S. history emphasize twentieth century. *Humanities,* March-April.

Wilentz, Sean. (1997). Don't know much about history: A battle report from the front lines in america's cultural wars. *New York Times Book Review,* November 30, 28–29.

Zabarenko, Deborah. (2001). U.S. census reports more multicultural population. *Reuters.* March 12.

Index